Passing Through

An Existential Journey Across America's Outback

Richard Menzies

Stephens Press, LLC
A *Las Vegas Review-Journal* Book

Richard Menzies Mar 2008

Photography: Richard Menzies, Editor: Sandy Knauke, Designer: Sue Campbell
Production Assistance: Maria Coccaro

ISBN: 1-932-173-40-4

CIP Data Available

Stephens
Press LLC

A Stephens Media Group Company
P.O. Box 1600, Las Vegas, Nevada 89125-1600

www.stephenspress.com

Printed in Hong Kong

Acknowledgements

No man is an island, not even in Nevada. The author is indebted to a number of people and institutions, beginning with the English Department of the University of Utah—which, by refusing to admit me as a student, forced me to venture out into the real world. I owe much to my longtime friend Richard Goldberger, whose bright idea it was to start a newspaper in Wendover and who introduced me to the likes of Floyd Eaton and Melvin Dummar. I am deeply indebted to Caroline J. Hadley and David Moore, past and present editors of *Nevada Magazine*, whose "assignments" over the years have given me a plausible excuse for hitting the road. Thanks also to Kenneth Donoghue, whose grant of $150 kept me in gas money for a time, and to Ray Walker, who sent me fifty bucks and a secondhand shirt.

The attendees and sponsors of the annual "Shooting the West" photography symposium in Winnemucca—in particular the Saturday night crowd—hold a special place in my heart. I'll never forget the time we shot up the town with Larry's Nikon.

Without the unflagging encouragement and support of my wife Anne, none of my impossible dreams would ever come true.

Finally, I am indebted to those citizens and denizens of the Great Basin who have so graciously shared their time and thoughts—and bestowed countless kindnesses upon this stranger who, after all, was only passing through.

— Richard Menzies

Out of a misty dream
Our path emerges for a while,
Then closes
Within a dream.

— Ernest Dowson

CONTENTS

CHAPTER ONE: *Going West* 8
Conan the Librarian, mild-mannered enforcer of Skull Valley's no-fly zone, encounters the colossus of Wendover and sees prehistoric flying reptiles in the night skies.

CHAPTER TWO: *Deputy Dump* 19
I become acquainted with the municipal dump's resident peace officer and learn the true identity of Elizabeth Taylor.

CHAPTER THREE: *Chief Thunder Speaks*........29
Running low on fuel, I stumble upon a roadside monument to The Great Spirit, constructed of native materials by a Native American visionary.

CHAPTER FOUR: *Footless And Fancy Free* 39
I used to think I had problems; then, I met a man who had no feet.

CHAPTER FIVE: *Two Car Bob* 49
Theodor "Bob" Heist lost his wife, quit his job, and drank himself to death—but not before getting a piece of the Great American Dream.

CHAPTER SIX: *Literati Of The Longest Road*..55
Carl Hayden and Tom Clay both lived alongside Highway 93; yet when it came to legalized gambling, they stood on opposite sides of the street.

CHAPTER SEVEN: *Lonely, Lonelier, Loneliest*.67
A serendipitous journey into the lonely heart of America's Outback, including lively encounters with reluctant immigrant Maria Pavlakis, much-traveled misfit Jack Killinger, and steel-driving man Louis Gibellini. In Austin, I sleep through an Indian uprising. In a remote desert valley north of Cold Springs Station I'm introduced to Ray Walker, a man with no problems.

CHAPTER EIGHT: *Sparks Of Genius* 87
Self-styled scientist Robert K. Golka ventured west in search of optimum ground conductivity. He should have brought more money.

CHAPTER NINE: *One Car Bob* 97
Down, but not yet out, Bob McKinney boldly grows where no gardener has grown before.

CHAPTER TEN: *Pennies From Heaven*...........103
Melvin Dummar yearned to see his name in lights, but all he got was a bit part in a movie about his life.

CHAPTER ELEVEN: *Going South* 113
I learn the "truth" about Deputy Dump and discover the stuff that dreams are made of.

AFTERWORD 121
Oops! I only *thought I had Deputy Dump figured out.*

The Great Salt Desert.
My job entailed tracking
down two or three dozen library
patrons dispersed over
4.5 million acres of
saline desolation.

Deputy Dump on duty.
"When I first come here,
people thought I was just a tramp."
— Floyd Eaton

Eaton's junkyard home
was built of secondhand
materials, filled with
cast-off furniture and
appliances and populated
by animal friends.

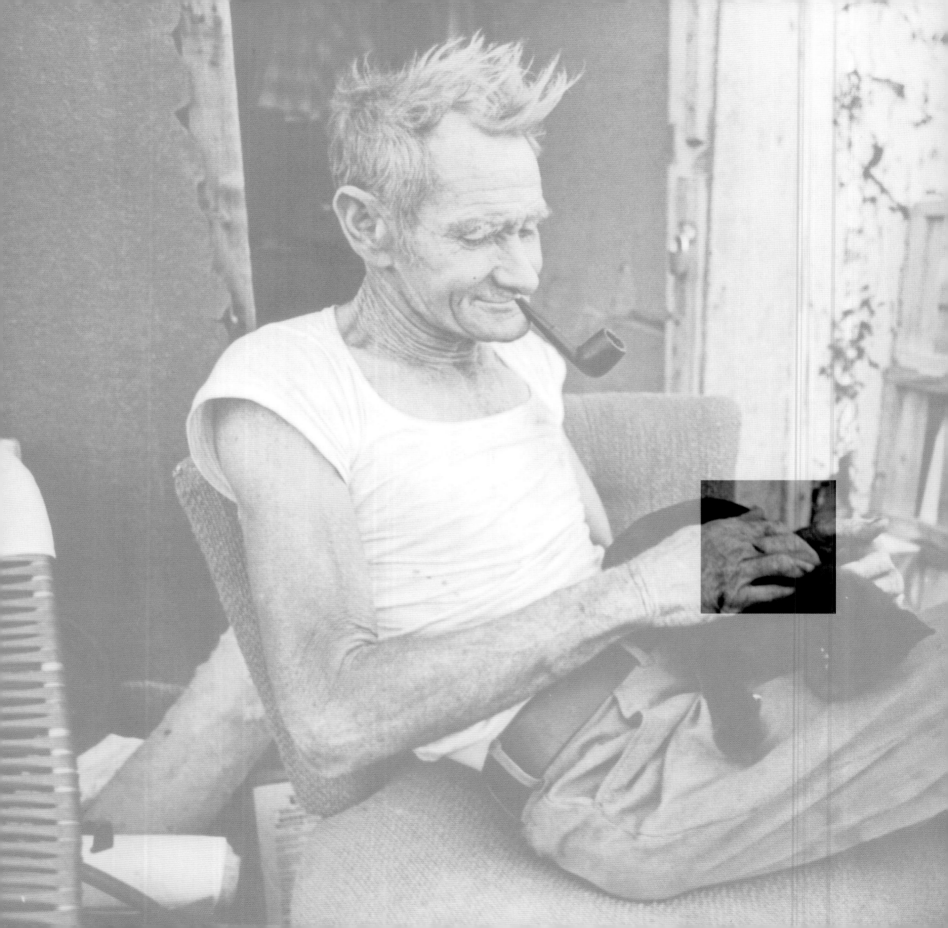

CHAPTER TWO

Deputy Dump

By the spring of 1970, Roy was well on the road to recovery and it was clear I would soon be out of a job. But I wasn't finished with Wendover. Something about those prehistoric reptiles soaring in the night sky and those shadowy figures flitting about Rippetoe's General Store had kindled my curiosity. I felt as if I had stumbled upon The Land That Time Forgot.

I'd also stumbled upon Floyd Eaton, better known around town as Deputy Dump. My first impression of the man remains a vivid one. Out of an acrid cloud of burning tire smoke he had emerged—tall and lean, the butts of a twin revolvers showing from a double shoulder holster. His thinning hair and pencil moustache were the color of the Kiwi-brand shoe polish he applied weekly. Into one corner of his toothless mouth was jammed a stubby Kaywoodie pipe. At his side was a black-and-white Border collie he called Tina—Deputy Dog.

Eaton, I learned, had resided in Wendover's municipal dump for six years, having ridden into town on horseback—or so he claimed.

"Come in here the head of a snowstorm out of Wells," he announced in a high-pitched Mississippi drawl. "Come out of Montana, the head of a snowstorm, stopped in Wells to see if there was any ranchers around there I could get a job with, ridin' range. Woke up one mornin', looked up on the hill, I says, 'Unh unh.'

"Big white cloud layin' right on the ground, low. I says, 'Here comes snow!' So I rode on in here."

We were chatting in Floyd's cabin, a ramshackle affair he'd constructed entirely from salvaged materials. All of his household furnishings had come off the dump as well, including his wood stove and easy chair, his bed, his kitchen table and chairs, his pots and pans, his knives and forks. His only possessions that hadn't previously been possessed by someone else were his cowboy hat and his pearl-buttoned shirt—items he insisted had been specially tailored to fit by Stockman's Western Wear in Denver. Then there was the badge.

Like its owner, it showed signs of hard use. Engraved on the front was an eagle perched upon a sunburst and below the sunburst was an inscription: *F. D. Eaton International Ranger.*

Who, I wondered, are the International Rangers?

"It's a international police association," Floyd explained, handing me a cup of thick, black coffee in a white ceramic cup I recognized as the same kind used in the StateLine Hotel and Casino coffee shop. "They got offices the world over."

"And you're a member?"

"Yep."

"Are you … an active member?"

"Semi-retired. You want anythang in your coffee?"

"Um, sugar and cream would be nice, if you have any."

"Got any ol' thang you want," Eaton sang out as he disappeared into the kitchen. When he returned, he was holding a complete serving set—creamer, sugar bowl, and a spoon—arranged upon a silvery platter.

"My, this is pretty fancy," I gushed. "Where did you get all this stuff? Did you bring it with you from Montana?"

"Texas," Eaton corrected. "No, all I had with me when I come was Tina, my Bible, and my guns. The rest of it all come right offa that hill. Come from the StateLine, most of it."

"And it all sort of matches," I marveled.

"Oh, the forks does. All the forks matches. But the knives and stuff don't. If I keep on, I'll get me a complete set yet."

"Why would they throw out perfectly good knives and forks?"

"They drop 'em in the garbage, wipin' the dishes and thangs off," Eaton explained. "Waitresses drops 'em in them garbage bags, and they just don't want to reach their little hands down in there and get it. Would you like a slice of pie?"

"No, thanks."

There followed a period of silence, during which nothing could be heard but the clink of spoon against porcelain, the drone of a greenbottle fly, a gentle sipping sound. Then a giant sucking sound as Eaton rekindled his Kaywoodie.

I was beginning to feel very much at home—and curiously safe. As a general rule, it's not the smartest thing to venture onto the compound of a heavily armed hermit; however, in Deputy Dump's custody, I sensed I was in good hands. Indeed, I was beginning to wonder if there might even be a particle of truth in his ridiculous claim that he was a lawman and not just another drifter who, most likely, had rolled into town in a boxcar.

Inquiring further, I learned that the International Rangers maintained a central office in Washington, D.C., and also a branch office in Mexico City. Eaton told me he had worked mostly out of the Mexico City office, adding that in all likelihood his superiors were desperately trying to get in touch with him. No doubt they had another murder for him to solve, an international dispute to settle, a notorious fugitive to capture. But Floyd Eaton was getting on in years and had wearied of the chase. Let someone else risk his fool neck, he declared. Colonel Eaton was effectively retired.

"*Colonel* Eaton?" I interjected.

"Uh huh."

Floyd took a sip of coffee and a meditative drag on his pipe. Another lengthy silence followed. I had the impression he was shuffling his mental cards, getting his "facts" in order.

"When I first come here," he resumed at last, "I didn't let nobody know that I was a officer. I kept that under my hat. There was people wondered—they seen me in town all the time—wondered why I carried a gun. But they never did ask me. Because there ain't no law, even in Utah, about carryin' a gun—so long as you carry it on the outside.

"Then Earl Lacy, he come here and took over as deputy sheriff. And after I got acquainted with him and found out what kind of a guy he was and ever'thang—why, then I introduced myself to him. Showed him my crudentials.

"He says, 'Hunh?' He just looked at 'em, and he handed 'em over to his father. And the old man, he looked at 'em.

"And I says, 'Now, if you ever need any help or anythang, you know who I am and where I'm at.' I says, 'All you gotta do is holler. I'll be glad to give you a hand, anytime day or night.'

"Earl, he says, 'Well, I'm glad to know that.' Says, 'I can use you a lotta times.'"

Eaton's position as self-appointed Elko County assistant deputy sheriff didn't pay anything, although it did have its fringe benefits. All the free WANTED posters Floyd could find room for on his cardboard walls, for instance, and also a fleet of unmarked patrol cars.

On any given day Deputy Dump's motor pool might number half a dozen vehicles—cars and trucks that had been found abandoned along Interstate 80 and impounded. After a certain period of time had lapsed and if the rightful owner hadn't showed up, the impounded vehicle became county property. Deputy Dump was then at liberty to drive it, once he had filled out and filed what he called the "resurrection papers."

Often after dark, Eaton could be seen patrolling the streets of Wendover in one of his resurrected cruisers, but his usual beat was the dump. He kept a watchful eye on the many vagrants and drunks who liked to "jungle up" in the shrubbery alongside the railroad tracks. If one of them should overstay his welcome, Eaton would advise him to catch the next freight out of town. Should he catch a hobo drinking, Floyd would "confisticate" his wine.

Most did as they were told once they saw the guns and the badge. But of course there will always be those who have no respect for authority.

"When I first come here," Floyd explained, "people thought I was just a tramp. And a guy used t' come out to the dump and shoot around. A couple of guys, they was up there shootin' around, shootin' at the stove pipe that stuck up outta my house.

"I stepped outside. Told 'em, I says, 'Boys, stop shootin' toward the house.' I says, 'I don't mind ya shootin' around, target practice, but don't be ashootin' toward the house.'

"'Aw, you old sonofabitch, what're you gonna do about it?' Says, 'What the fuck are you gonna do about it?'

"I says, 'I kin shoot *back*.'

"'*Shoot* back!' he says. 'See if we give a fuck!'

"Well, I had one of them forty-fours in my hand. I rocked the hammer back and put two of them two-hundred-and-forty-grain slugs up through them tin cans. And, boy, they tore out in that car, gettin' the hell away—I mean, they throwed gravel up clear t' the highway.

"So they went up and they seen Earl. They talked to Earl Lacy, and Earl says, 'You *what*?' Earl told 'em, he says, 'Look, boys, I wanna live just a little while. I'm not ready to die *yet*.' Says, 'I wouldn't go out there even in the daytime and start shootin' around, without lettin' that old man know somethin' about it.'

"They says, 'Why?'

"Earl, he says, 'You boys are just lucky he took pity and didn't hit you.'

"One of 'em says, 'Well, maybe he cain't shoot straight.'

"Earl says, 'Don't kid yerself. I saw him . . . *do* it.' Says, 'I personally seen that old man with my own eyes, standin' out there with them guns in their holsters and a box of clay pigeons. He'd take a clay pigeon in each hand and sail 'em up in the air, and he can draw them goddamn guns and break 'em!

"'So don't kid yerself. The old man can shoot, and he'd rather shoot you than look at ya.'"

"Wow . . ."

The picture Floyd painted seemed strangely familiar. When I was a boy, I'd spent many a Saturday afternoon at the local movie house, enthralled by the adventures of Hopalong Cassidy, Roy Rogers, Gene Autry, the Lone Ranger, and Lash LaRue. Just like Floyd, they were all fast on the draw. But they never shot to kill—not the first shot, anyway. No, the first shot was always a warning, a demonstration of superior marksmanship that either ventilated the bad guy's hat or else zapped the pistol cleanly from his hand.

I wondered aloud whether shooting clay pigeons out of the sky with a handgun was a skill Floyd had acquired as an International Ranger—or was it a stunt he'd copied from a movie?

"I *been* in a movie," Eaton interrupted.

"You have? And what movie was that?"

"The Giant."

"*Giant*? The one with Rock Hudson and . . . "

"Liz Taylor. Jane Wyman."

"Jane Wyman was in it?"

"Uh huh. You remember where Jane Wyman walked up and told that Mexican that she would take *that* horse? And that Mexican told her he didn't think it was a good idea, that it was the same horse that had just throwed Pedro?"

"You were Pedro? Or the Mexican?"

"No! I was Jane Wyman."

"Jane Wyman?"

"Yep. I was . . . I were that person."

"*You* were Jane Wyman?"

"Uh huh. You know, Jane Wyman was supposed to ride that horse, and it throwed and killed her. Well, I was the man that rode the horse. Instead of Jane Wyman."

My mind was racing. I had seen *Giant* several times, but couldn't remember Jane Wyman being in it. But there was a Jane somebody. Jane . . . *Withers*! And the movie *had been* filmed on location somewhere in East Texas. Was it Marfa?

"Yep, right there at Valentine," Floyd nodded. "I was there, I was workin' in the carnival. There was people runnin' around all over the place, and one guy come up and said, 'Goddamn, I've looked; I'm *lookin'* t' find somebody, but I can't find him.'

"I says, 'Who ya lookin' fer?' Says, 'I happen to be an investigator, maybe I kin help ya.'

"'I'm lookin' for somebody to ride a horse,' he says. 'I can't find no bronc riders.'

"I says, 'How old a horse?'

"He says, 'He's three years old.'

"I says, 'I've never seen a three-year-old horse yet I was ever afraid of.'

"He stopped and looked at me. He says, '*You* can ride a horse?'

"I says, 'Sure I kin ride a horse.' Says, 'I happen to be the guy that used to go by the name The Concho Kid.'

"He scratched his head. He says, 'Stay right here!' And goddamn, he was *gone*! Them long laigs of his, they was reachin' way out yonder. He was gone about five minutes, and directly, he come back. 'Come on here,' he says.

"Well, I went with him. And the guy says, 'Come in here. Come right in here and set down!'

"I walked over there under a canvas shell—the shade that they had. Set down in a chair. Directly, here come a guy out. He says, 'I'll make a woman outta ya.'

"He didn't even take my sideburns or moustache or nothin' off. He left 'em on, but he fixed 'em so you couldn't see 'em. Then he put a long brown wig on. He put that wig on me and give me a shirt to put on. Then I rolled my pant legs up and put that damned skirt on. He looked at me, he says, 'Let's see!'

"'Hell,' he says, 'he looks just like her!' Says, 'That boy looks just like Jane; he'd pass for her twin sister.' He says, 'C'mon, boy! You wanna look the script over?'

"I says, 'Do I gotta say anythang? Just tell me what I gotta say. I can remember.'

"He told me what I had to say, and when the time come, why, he give me the highball.

"And I says, 'Jiminy Christ, I'll show you people how to do thangs.' I walked over, I says, 'Gimme a horse!' And I looked around, I says, 'I'll take *that* one!'

"The Mexican, he says, 'No, Señora, I do not think so. De horse, he jus' throw Pedro.'

CHAPTER THREE

Chief Thunder Speaks

U.S. Interstate 80 is the main road across Nevada—the road most traveled and the one visitors most likely have in mind when they lament that the Silver State is naught but a vast sagebrush wasteland.

The interstate runs roughly parallel to the Emigrant Trail, the same route California-bound wagon trains followed in the nineteenth century. Spaced at generous intervals along the way are towns named Winnemucca, Wells, Elko, Lovelock, Battle Mountain, Golconda, and Oasis. Why did some pioneers choose to stop at such godforsaken places instead of pressing on to palmy California? Most likely because their oxen died or the wheels fell off their wagons. Or, as in the case of Chief Rolling Mountain Thunder, their engines quit.

I first met Chief Thunder in the summer of 1973. By that time, I had been let go from my librarian job and was working as feature editor of the upstart tabloid the *Salt Flat News*. In a borrowed station wagon, I had driven from my home in Salt Lake City to Reno, where I had arranged to meet Charles Carpenter, a brakeman for the Western Pacific railroad and an avid weekend prospector. Part-time prospectors aren't uncommon in Nevada, but Carpenter stood out because instead of panning for flakes and nuggets he panned for wedding rings.

It so happens that Reno, being the divorce capital of the United States, also leads the nation in the production of cast-off wedding rings. Many can be seen on display in the windows of the pawnshops that line Commercial Row, but a small percentage wind up at the bottom of the Truckee River—tossed there, according to legend, by jubilant divorcees.

I found it hard to believe anyone would actually throw away gold jewelry, but evidently it's true. In three weekend outings, Carpenter had recovered half a dozen wedding bands from the gravel underneath the Virginia Street Bridge. He'd also brought up a number of coins, an assortment of trinkets, and one wristwatch.

My interview with Carpenter proved to be most difficult. To begin with, he and his two-man crew operated a small dredge that was powered by an unmuffled gasoline engine. The engine's roar, combined with the rumble of traffic passing overhead on Reno's busiest thoroughfare, made conversation all but impossible.

Just to get within shouting distance of my subject proved challenging. First, I had to hike several hundred feet upstream from the bridge until I found an opening in the flood wall that borders the river. From there, I was obliged to wade downstream in knee-deep water, picking my way over slippery rocks while holding aloft my camera in one hand and my cassette tape recorder in the other.

Once underneath the bridge, I discovered I could scarcely make out a word Carpenter was saying. To complicate matters, a crowd of onlookers had gathered along the bridge railing. Pennies, nickels, pebbles and spittle rained down upon my head. I shook my fist and roared like the Billy Goat Gruff, but to no effect.

Interview concluded, I thanked Carpenter for taking the time to talk to me. "What?" he shouted, looking up from his sluice box and cupping an ear.

"I need to be going now," I shouted. "Thanks very much for the interview!"

"Unh." Charles Carpenter grunted and went back to sifting the sediment in search of buried sentiment.

I passed the next hour or so pulling slot machine handles in the hope that I, too, might strike pay dirt in "The Biggest Little City in the World." Before I realized what was happening, I was flat broke.

Downtown Reno isn't the most pleasant place to hang out when your pockets are empty and your sneakers soaking wet. All you can do is stand in a doorway, watch as the tragic pageantry of humanity files past, and try hard to pretend that you're not a part of it. The majority of the passers-by looked to be retirees in the process of switching casinos. Each carried a cocktail glass in one hand and a paper coin cup in the other. Picture an army of organ grinder's monkeys, all outfitted in double-knit cardigan sweaters and purple polyester pantsuits.

An elderly man shuffled past, wearing a sandwich board advertising Joe's Pawn Shop. On a nearby curb sat a young man, holding his head in his hands and weeping. A transient approached, introduced himself as Eddie, and offered to sell me a "fun packet" of coupons redeemable at Mr. Sy's House of Fun in Las Vegas for two dollars. I told him I'd just about had my fill of "fun."

From within the gilded gates of Harrah's doorway sounded the clamor of bells and whistles signifying sudden, unmerited prosperity. Money, money everywhere, but not a cent for me!

Luckily, I hadn't pawned my borrowed station wagon, and there remained enough gasoline in the tank to get me as far as Lovelock. There, a filling station attendant took pity on me and loaned me two dollars worth of gas—enough to get me to Winnemucca, where there was a station that would honor my Husky Oil credit card.

I was about halfway between Lovelock and Winnemucca, at a dot on the roadmap called Imlay, when I spied something most unusual. Standing three stories tall and ornately decorated, it somewhat resembled a tiered wedding cake. Drawing closer, I saw that it was a building, with walls that were a conglomeration of concrete and rocks, wine bottles, beer cans, railroad ties, antlers, pipe, angle iron, automobile wheels, chicken wire, and hubcaps. Along the eaves ran a fanciful bas-relief frieze. Atop the roof stood a statuary garden, entwined in a tangle of colorful hoops and arches.

I exited the highway and proceeded toward the place, slowly. Along the way I passed a stern-visaged stone figure wearing nothing but a loincloth and holding a cross to his belly.

"**Welcome To The Thunder Mountain Museum**" read a sign painted in shaky freehand. "**No Unleased (sic) Pets Allowed**" read another. "**No Tresspassing** (sic)" read still another.

Still I pressed onward, uncertain how many taboos I might be violating and with a mounting sense of dread not unlike what General Custer must have felt the day he rode out to Little Big Horn.

I passed what looked to be a subdivision of daub and bottle huts in various stages of construction. I waved at a long-haired worker in overalls whose skin was the color of Portland cement, but got no response.

I came to a rusty ore cart piled high with bleached bones. Spray-painted on the side of the cart was a single word: "Promises."

I had begun to look for a spot to turn around when I was approached by a pert young woman who reminded me somewhat of the Charles Manson disciple Lynette "Squeaky" Fromme. I'll call her Squeaky, since I don't remember the name she gave me, which in all likelihood wasn't her *real* name, anyway.

Squeaky appeared delighted to have company. Although her mud dwelling stood right next to an interstate highway, she rarely had visitors.

"I think it's a case of museum worry," she confided.

"Is that what this place is?" I asked. "A museum?"

"Sort of," Squeaky answered. "It's also a spiritual retreat, but Chief Rolling Mountain Thunder calls it The Monument."

Squeaky led me to the monument's owner and chief architect. Tall, dark, and handsome, Chief Thunder cut an imposing figure in spite of the thrift shop clothes he wore. Through the open neck of his boiled felt shirt I could make out the ribbed collars of at least two pairs of insulated undershirts. His outermost layer consisted of a torn, oil-stained jacket, baggy khakis, and steel-toed work boots. Crowning his head was a jaunty cap from which sprouted a single eagle feather.

In one hand he held a mason jar filled with a brownish liquid I guessed was either black coffee or motor oil. In his shirt pocket was a pack of Lark cigarettes. A lit Lark smoldered between his lips, an unlit spare was tucked behind his left ear. All during our visit—in fact, every time I ever saw him—Chief Thunder was never without a pack of cigarettes in his pocket, a lit cigarette in his mouth, a spare behind his ear, and a mason jar filled with brownish liquid in his hand.

He told me he was a full-blooded Creek Indian and a decorated combat veteran of World War II. Before coming to Nevada, he'd worked in California as a law enforcement officer. In those days he'd gone by his Anglo name—Frank Van Zant. In his heart of hearts, however, he'd never been anyone other than Chief Rolling Mountain Thunder.

As if he had all the time in the world, Chief Thunder showed me around the compound—five acres littered with boards and bed springs, spools of bailing wire, odd pieces of pipe, rebar, rusted out pickup trucks and cannibalized cars, water heaters, railroad ties, cast iron boilers, a vintage Coca-Cola machine, a cow skull, a typewriter, tattered sofas of Mediterranean design. Amid the clutter I spotted a doll and a tricycle—playthings belonging to Chief Thunder's son, Thunder Mountain Thunder, and his young daughter, Obsidian Lightning Thunder.

Many questions were racing through my mind. I began by asking the chief where, exactly, the museum was.

"That's the question I'm asked the most," he answered. "People ask, 'Where's the museum?' They've already passed a thousand feet of Americana and artifacts, and they're stumbling over 'em, and they wonder where the museum is. If it's not an artifact, if it isn't an antique, if it's not in a glass case, then it's not a museum."

I nodded as if to indicate that I understood. I next asked if he could explain what Squeaky had meant by the term "museum worry."

"Most people come here," said the chief, "they don't even want to come in. They stop at the front gate and that's as far as they get. What's happens to many of 'em, they get museum weary."

"Oh, *weary*." I scratched out the word worry on my reporter's notepad and wrote the word weary.

"Yes," Thunder continued. "There is a saying amongst museum curators that people get 'museum worry.' They get tired; it wears 'em out. And I think they get to that point before they even get to the door here. That was another thing I was warned about by the American Museum Association twenty, thirty years ago—never have too much stuff on the outside. 'Cause they'll see too much, and they'll get that museum worry."

Chief Thunder paused to take a sip of the brown liquid and to light up a fresh cigarette. I scratched out the word weary on my notepad and rewrote worry.

I ventured an opinion that another drawback to having too much valuable stuff lying around is that visitors might be tempted to walk off with it. But Chief Thunder said he never worried about that. The average American, he insisted, is incapable of telling what's valuable from what isn't. An arrowhead he might notice, but he'll walk right past an ordinary rock lying on the ground and fail to recognize the significance of it because it's not behind glass in a display case.

"Like that old 1913 automobile wheel over there," he said. "Why, it looks far more natural leaning up against a fence than it would in a case. And what's the point of looking at several hundred of the same type of arrow points? One will do it; one point is enough. You can associate it immediately with the area it belongs in—then it'll mean something."

Thunder's argument made sense to me. In fact, I was beginning to wonder whether Charles Carpenter might be committing an archeological offense by dredging up all those cast-off wedding bands. Better he should leave those symbols of failed matrimony where they belong—*in situ*, on the rocks.

Chief Thunder impressed me as a man very much at home in his environment. He didn't cultivate. He didn't irrigate. He hadn't tried to electrify the darkness, nor had he felt compelled to erect a structure evocative of some exotic land. Just as the pioneers had built sod houses on the prairie and log cabins in the woods, Thunder had built his dwelling using materials indigenous to the American roadside. Moreover, he'd put it all together without benefit of a blueprint, relying instead for guidance from The Great Spirit.

He told me he'd first come to Imlay in 1959, not long after taking leave of his law enforcement job in order to embark upon what Indians call a vision quest.

"We spent ten days on the mountain and researched it enough to know that it was *the* mountain—the Thunder Mountain of legend," he explained. "That craggy one up there, it was the spirit mountain or God mountain or something like that long before the white man came here. It was a spirit place, and it was the place where some people wanted to be buried. And then on the other side of it, between Thunder Mountain and Star Peak, why, they had the sacred meeting grounds where they met for thousands of years even before the Paiutes came in."

In Sacred Canyon, the chief said, he had uncovered a projectile point datable to 11,000 B.C. and also a petrified human footprint that was over a million years old.

Even back then, according to Chief Thunder, Pershing County was looked upon as a wasteland.

"The ancient man, all he used it for was a piece of geography to get from one place to the other. If a rabbit got in his way, he might shoot it, but he didn't live on the land, he didn't hunt on it. And the white man today doesn't; he just goes shootin' through."

Thunder withdrew a fresh Lark cigarette from his shirt pocket, slipped it between his lips and lit it from the smoldering butt he held in his fingers. Then he flicked the butt into the sagebrush, inhaled deeply, and squinted in the direction of the highway the United States Automobile Association has dubbed the deadliest in America.

"*I* never considered *living* here," he continued, "because it was too much work, and I was too old *then*. And eight years later, why, circumstances, visions and everything—I found myself right back here on this mountain, eight years older and doing it anyway.

"So I built that one place one mile up the canyon, and I thought that was enough. And I started to leave. I was just going to drive away and leave it, only I couldn't get away. I got forced back with a full load, and there was a car sitting here on the prairie. I stopped and asked if they needed any help, and it was the guy who owned the property. And he offered me such terms that I couldn't turn it down."

What did he mean, I wondered, by 'forced back'?

"I couldn't get down the road. I got as far as Carson City, and the car began to die and quit. Wouldn't run anymore, and we didn't have the money to afford a big repair bill, so we turned around and started back this way, and it ran perfectly."

Chief Thunder's account of how the Thunder Mountain Museum came to be squared nicely with my theory that vehicular breakdown is the motivating force behind all northern Nevada settlements. The twist was that Thunder's car ran well enough in the vicinity of Imlay. It might even take him as far as Reno—that is, provided he was only going into town in order to pick up groceries or another load of cement. But just try making a break for California and the wheels would fall off! The Great Spirit works in mysterious ways.

Thunder continued: "When I bought these two canyons up here and started scruffing in them, I thought, that's where He wants us to live. But He lets us get places started up there, and then He just makes it impossible for me to work in there. And then somebody else moves in. So I guess we're just opening it up for these people who are interested in living the old, traditional ways."

The chief placed the current population of Thunder Mountain at eight or nine—counting himself, his children, and his attractive young wife, Ahtrum. His extended family included Squeaky and Dale, the reticent hippie mason, plus two or three others. I was told there was a reclusive Ph.D. holed up in a cave in Sacred Canyon, and an elderly Indian medicine woman sequestered somewhere inside the labyrinthine Monument.

"And we have one who's an attorney, a female attorney, and she's building her own place. She's doing some writing and other things. On very special occasions, she enters this ground, but we don't enter her place and she don't enter ours.

"Each has his own lodge and he's expected to stay in it. Nobody enters another's abode unless it's a real emergency. We work together all day, but at night, when the day's work is done, everybody goes to their own rooms, and that's where they're expected to stay.

"It's pretty rough, and the average person couldn't take it. But we don't ask them to work; nobody is asked to work here. The only thing we ask is that they don't interfere with those who are working."

I wondered how such a diverse assortment of pilgrims managed to find the place. Had Thunder placed an ad in the Whole Earth catalog? Distributed flyers on the campus of San Francisco State University? Placed a hex on the carburetors of northern Nevada?

Chief Thunder took a long, deep drag on what was left of his cigarette. He patted his shirt pocket, then reached behind his ear for the emergency spare. Once it was safely lit, he dispatched little Obsidian Lightning Thunder to the house to fetch a fresh carton.

"Most of 'em," he resumed, "just fall in off the road. Some just seem to know exactly what it is, especially those who've worked hard in their life. They know what it is, and foreigners seem to know—people from the old country, people from England and those places. Italians, they seem to know exactly what it is.

"The only qualifications we've ever had is that they aspire to the pure and radiant heart. That doesn't mean they have to be pure and radiant—there's no such thing—only that they would like to be a little bit more pure and have a little more radiant heart than they have, you know, and be willing to work for it."

Thunder answered my last question even before I asked it. Yes, there was a vacancy on the grounds, in the nearly completed Temple of the Wind. If I wished, I could have it all to myself, rent-free, for as long as I wanted. No security or cleaning deposits. No references, no background check.

It was a tempting offer. After all, I was not only penniless but still relatively rootless, and it occurred to me that "Temple of the Wind" would look pretty good on my business card. On the downside, I doubted that journalism would qualify as a "pure and radiant" pursuit. And, of course, I also had reservations about moving into a house made of junk, out in the middle of nowhere, surrounded by neighbors of dubious mental stability. In sum, I was consumed with museum worry.

I thanked Chief Thunder for the generous offer, promising that I'd think it over. As a parting gift, he offered me an antique cash register.

"Oh, no," I protested. "I couldn't. Something like that must be worth a lot of money."

As I pulled away from Thunder Mountain, it dawned on me that I had a long way yet to go before achieving spiritual enlightenment. No, I was still very much a captive of materialism. I had put a price on a priceless gift and turned down a free room in the Temple of the Wind. And *now* what? I was just another worrywart rolling along the interstate, with one eye on the fuel gauge and a prayer in my not-so-radiant heart that my tank wouldn't run dry before I got to Winnemucca.

"Actually, I'll tell you. I finally realized after fifteen years that what I'm doin' along the highway is runnin' a nonprofit counseling service."

— Stanley Gurcze

CHAPTER FOUR

Footless and Fancy Free

In September 1973, I said goodbye to cheap motel rooms and bought myself a brand new Volkswagen campmobile. A bright orange one, with louvered side windows and a rear seat that converts into a bed. The spartan living room includes a sink and icebox, a foldaway table, an overhead shelf, a single drawer, and a tiny closet. In addition, there are curtains that can be drawn across all the windows, thus affording complete privacy in even the most public of places. Thirty years later, I'm still driving it.

Best of all, no matter how far from home I wander, at night I always return to the same place. Whether parked in the Tuscarora graveyard or sandwiched between idling semis at the King Eight Truck Stop in Las Vegas, I find comfort in familiar surroundings.

With only thirteen percent of its land surface privately owned, Nevada abounds in potential camping sites. Nevertheless, I'm particular about where I choose to stop for the night. I take care not to stray into Indian territory or onto military reservations, and I almost never rest at roadside rest areas, where noise levels and crime rates rival those of the inner city.

My rule has but one exception—a rest area named Moor, which lies just off Interstate 80 about ten miles east of Wells. Many are the restful nights I've passed there, railroad tracks on one side, four-lane freeway on the other. Yet no one has ever pulled alongside to disturb my slumber. Come morning, there are never fresh tire tracks in the crusty soil, nor new trash in the trash barrel. I very much doubt the Nevada highway department is even aware that a rest stop at Moor exists.

Not far away from my usual camping spot stands a bower of piñon trees enclosing what looks to be a hobo camp. The furnishings include a car seat upholstered in peeling Naugahyde, in front of which stands a plywood cable spool cum coffee table. On top of the table a plastic fork lies beside an empty can of Chef Boyardee brand spaghetti.

Some clothing—slacks, shirts, sneakers, and a worn pair of cowboy boots—are stashed nearby in a cardboard box, and in a small clearing is a twin-size mattress. Originally from a child's bedroom, the mattress is patterned with images from the television series *Star Trek*.

In a nearby ravine lies a Zenith television set, flat on its back with its picture tube shot out. So one of the things you can't do during a layover at Moor is watch television. What you can do is sit on your Naugahyde car seat sofa eating cold spaghetti from a can. Or else you can stretch out on the mattress, alongside Captain Kirk and Mister Spock, gaze up at the heavens and think deep thoughts.

I confess I've passed more than a few hours doing just that— yet no time at all compared to Mr. Stanley Gurcze, whose social security number included the digits O-O-7. "My license," he explained, "to kill time."

I met Stanley on the outskirts of Elko in September of the bicentennial year, 1976. I was on my way home from Mountain Home, Idaho, where I'd gone to interview John Bloomer—founder, president, and sole employee of the Bloomer Flying Saucer Company. Bloomer had shown me a scale model of the circular aircraft he intended to build. Powered by four big block Chevy V-8 engines, it would be capable of lifting straight up off the shag carpeting of Bloomer's living room, then cruising at supersonic speed into the kitchen, where John's wife, Marlies, looked on apprehensively.

On an impulse, I had decided to return home via State Route 51—a spectacularly lonely byway that runs southward from Mountain Home across a barren plain dotted here and there with sagebrush and the occasional pronghorn.

Near Mountain City I had pulled over for the night, but found it hard to sleep amid such quietude. Shortly before dawn I finally gave up, slithered from my sleeping bag into the driver's seat, and continued south through the Humboldt National Forest. Presently thunder rumbled overhead and raindrops began to pelt my windshield.

Rounding a bend, I spied two shadowy forms huddled beside the road. It was a teenaged boy and girl, both wearing bedraggled turbans—and of course I had no choice but to stop and pick them up, because by now it was raining hard and mine was most likely the only car they'd see all morning.

I unlatched and pushed open the sliding cargo door. "Jump in!" I shouted.

The pair nodded gratefully and clambered aboard. "We're Sikhs," they announced in unison.

"Well, great. And what might you two be sikhing out here in the middle of nowhere?"

"Nothing, here. We're on our way to Sedona, Arizona. Sikhs from all over the country are gathering there. It's an ideal place to commune with nature."

"And no doubt better suited for your clothes than northern Nevada," I said. "Would you care for a cup of tea?"

As I went about drawing water from the holding tank and lighting the butane burner, the pair looked on with rapt expressions, as if beholding for the first time the sacred water-heating ritual.

Once teatime was over, the three of us continued south. They asked where I was bound, and I told them Elko. One thing I've learned is to never tell a hitchhiker how far you're actually going. That way if you should tire of his company, you'll have a ready-made excuse for letting him off at the earliest opportunity.

I was relieved when at last the modest skyline of Elko came into view. By then I'd had a surfeit of Sikhism. Clearly, Arizona was in for it, in terms of stimulating conversation.

I let the pair out in front of the Mayfair market on Idaho Street, with a parting suggestion that they stock up on food and water before resuming their pilgrimage. Then I drove off, circled the block, returned to Idaho Street, and headed east toward the city limits. I passed the two teenaged Sikhs, who evidently had ignored my advice and already were standing beside the road with their thumbs out. Their mouths dropped as I sped past, eyes fixed straight ahead.

On the outskirts of Elko was assembled a veritable *mob* of hitchhikers. Almost all wore long hair and carried guitar cases—the sort that tend to view Volkswagen microbuses like mine as a form of free public transit. But I didn't stop; I didn't even slow down, and in my rearview mirror I watched as peace signs morphed into middle-finger salutes. I didn't care; I was facing a long stretch of open road, and the only voice I was in the mood to hear now was that of Gordon Lightfoot on my tape player.

I had traveled another two miles when I spied it—a squat, rectangular shape by the side of the road, scarcely taller than a sagebrush. Thinking it might be a parcel that had fallen from a truck, I eased my foot off the accelerator. As I flashed past, I could see that "the thing" was alive.

It was a man, a very short one. A man with no legs, sitting—or was he kneeling? He hadn't been holding his thumb out, but what else would he be doing but trying to hitch a ride?

Another mile rolled past before I realized I had no choice but to turn around and investigate. The stubby stranger hadn't moved an inch, but remained firmly planted as a statue.

I stopped the car and stepped out. "Would you like a ride?" I asked.

The stranger looked me up and down; I had the odd sensation it was he who was bestowing the favor.

"Yes, thank you," he answered. "I would."

His name, he said, was Stanley Gurcze, and he was 59 years of age. When I asked where he was headed, he told me Mount Rushmore. It was the same thing he would tell everyone who asked him where he was bound in the year 1976.

Where was he from? Cleveland, he said. How long had he been on the road? Fifteen years, he said. *Fifteen* years?

I stole a second look at my passenger. Clearly, he had spent a good deal of time in the out-of-doors. His skin was the color and texture of shoe leather, and even the whites of his eyes weren't exactly white. He emitted a pungent body odor that informed me he hadn't showered in a long, long time.

The significant detail about the hitchhiker Stanley Gurcze, however, was the fact he had no feet. Both legs ended just below his kneecaps, which were covered with thick leather pads.

This must be the king of all hitchhikers, I thought—a vagabond without peer! I wanted very much to hear his story, and—lucky for me—Stan was in a talkative mood. He began by answering the question he'd most frequently been asked during his fifteen-year-long walkabout:

"My legs? I froze 'em off, just playin' out in the snow. I was ten years old. Cleveland, Ohio. But you know, there's no way to keep a ten-year-old kid indoors when the snow is out there, beautiful snowdrifts in every direction. So I put on a pair of tennis shoes, and I went outside and played all day.

"Well, that wind comin' up offa Lake Erie gets cold. And it's a moist cold; it goes right through ya. When I first started playin', my feet were cold, but then they started warmin' up, and I didn't know what the heck that meant. Then when they got real nice and comfortable, they were frozen. Ha ha. I didn't know that. But I sure found out, the next morning.

"But my mother, she came from Poland and she had these old-fashioned ideas. That if God wants him to die, let him die in peace. Big deal, you know. It's *my* life—but she had these ideas. So it took my other relatives thirty days—a month—to convince her to sign that permission for the first operation. And by that time, gangrene'd set in. So, two years later I got outta the hospital.

"Oh, I had artificial legs for awhile. I've worn out about eight pairs of artificial legs. I used to run, dance, play football, play baseball—everything else. But my last leg fell apart in Durango, Colorado. I got caught in a rainstorm—slept in the rain all night—and that leg got soakin' wet. It was just made outta laminated leather and four rivets. All glued together, you know.

"I had a dollar in my pocket, and I saw a grocery store down't the bottom of the hill. Started walkin' down there to get somethin' to eat. I'll tell ya, I didn't take only about fifty steps and my leg *exploded*! Just fell apart. That was fourteen years ago, and I been on my knees ever since.

"Well, the only reason I use crutches is, all this ground's uneven. I might step on a sharp rock with this right knee, but with the crutches I can favor it. But indoors, I never use crutches. As long as I don't have to walk on this doggone gravel and broken glass and everything else.

"My knees aren't calloused, either. Because whatdyacallit—the kneecap, *patella*, is just movin' all the time, so there's no way to get a callous on the knee. But I can get a blister on my shins. I got six inches of shin on this one, and seven over here. So I'm always off balance. Use every muscle in my body. Then these pad things move back and forth, and before I know it, I got a blister where it rubs. Then I say, 'Hey, you're handicapped!' Sonofagun! Surprise, surprise. Ha ha. 'What the hell are you doin' here?' Can't do nothin' about it.

"What could I do? *Nothin'*, good heavens! Oh, I worked, doin' assembly work, soldering. Which is an obsolete skill right now—they spot-weld everything now. I worked at it eleven years, took the same bus every day, saw the same people. But after my mother and older brother passed away, why, I just got on the highway. That was 1961. *Fif-teen* years ago.

"Oh, the first coupla years, I'd just go from town to town, you know, lookin' for work. I'd stop at employment offices. I used to have one leg on—one artificial leg—so I was halfway presentable. But I could usually only get work cleanin' up around truck stops, washin' dishes—stuff like that. Labor.

"But when I got on my knees, I'd hear about a job and go ask for it, and the man would say, 'No, I really didn't have a job. I was only kidding.'

"But I learned, *indirectly*, the reason they said that was because they were afraid of what the neighbors would think. They'd worry the neighbors would say they're takin' advantage of me, see. Bein' on my knees. So as a consequence, hell, I couldn't work. Couldn't work, I couldn't eat. So I keep travelin'.

"I don't know—maybe I'm not *tall* enough to work. I used to walk into personnel managers' offices, but they'd look at me kinda shocked. I'd ask for a job, and they'd go through a pretense of lookin' through their files, and then come back, say, 'No sir, we don't have anything for you.' 'Only for able-bodied men,' they'd say.

"And then in other cases, rather than say 'able-bodied men,' they'd say, 'Well, how *old* are you?'

"And I'd tell 'em, and they'd say, 'Well, we're looking for *younger* people.' Oh, *boy*. Literally pat me on the head and . . .

"Well, you know, people are funny. I don't know why, but many people I meet have the strangest idea that anybody that's *physically* handicapped is *mentally* handicapped. It's true. But they don't realize that any person that's handicapped tries harder than an able-bodied person. To accomplish more in any field. Hell, I can do anything anybody else can.

"But I'm not lookin' for work now. Naw, I gave that up already. 'Cause I've run inta so many excuses. I've heard every excuse there is, and the hell with it. Besides, I only got three more years to go and I'll be eligible for Social Security. I've got three years to get to where I'm headin'. No matter where I'm goin', I've got three years to get there.

"I enjoy being all by myself out in the middle of nowhere. 'Cause I've been a loner all my life, anyway. I'm on the road 49 weeks a year, and maybe four or five times in a year I can get lucky and get a motel room for the night. Where I can take a bath and wash my clothes. Of course, they're never dry in the morning, so I gotta put 'em on damp, and I try to dry 'em as I walk along the highway. And I have to sleep on the floor. Beds are too soft for me; even when I go home, I can't sleep on a bed. I've gotta put some rocks and broken bottles in the mattress to give it some *body*.

"But I never worry about how many steps it's gonna take me to get from here to there. I know I'm gonna get there eventually. Might be today or tomorrow—might be next week. I don't worry about it; I'm not in a hurry. I tell people I'm on my way to see Mount Rushmore now, but my plans are always subject to change at a moment's notice. I say I have an *idea* I wanna see Mount Rushmore;

I'm headin' in that general direction. But whether I get there this year or not, I don't care.

"The only time I ever get in a rush is when I start headin' for Cleveland, Ohio, after the snow melts there in the spring. Then I make a sign and put it on my back. And so help me, I get in a car and the man'll say, 'Where you headin' for?'

"It says *Ohio* on the sign, but he says, 'Where you headin' for?' And sometimes I get very antisocial, and I hide the sign. I say the hell with it—*guess* where the hell I'm goin'!

"I usually go back home for three weeks, but I don't know, maybe next year I might just write 'em a letter. I don't like that Yankee country anyway. It's just too hard to get a ride there. And I'm too stubborn to accept a bus ticket from Cleveland to Saint Louis, where I can get across the Mississippi and back inta God's country.

"You know, the attitudes of the people change just like that, from black to white. On the west side of the Mississippi, you can walk up to anybody and say, 'Good morning!' They'll smile, they'll answer you. You do the same thing east of the Mississippi River—even in East Saint Louis, right across the river—say 'Good morning, sir,' and he gets that very suspicious expression on his face as if to say, 'Now, why did he say good morning to me? What's he tryin' to get outta me?'

"See, they have that suspicious mind. That's the way they're brought up. That's why I don't like that part of the country.

"Besides, it's too crowded back there. There's too many dadgum Yankees. All of them towns, most of them towns on the old highways are only five miles apart. There's no place to camp out, no place to build a fire or nothin.' You build a fire, within five or ten minutes you have a deputy sheriff to talk to. And he thinks you're tryin' to burn down the state or something.

"Another thing, all you see east of the Mississippi River, you see a curve or a hill and trees on both sides. You can't see nothin.'

But out here, I can see where I'm gonna be in about thirty or forty minutes. Just look straight ahead.

"But when I go home to see my relatives, I sit in that room, I look at three walls. You know, people keep sayin', 'Well, I sit there and I look at the four walls.' They never think, they can't see the one *behind* 'em. Ha ha.

"I get a kick out of a lotta these Texans. I say, 'How long you been living here?' They say, 'I been livin' here *all* my life.' I say, 'Friend, you haven't *lived* all your life yet.' They never think of simple things like that.

"See, I have a different perspective. As short as I am—four feet, two-and-a-half inches, by the way—I still weigh two hundred pounds. I'm wide. I think my bones weigh a hundred and ninety-eight pounds. But when I was workin' I weighed two hundred and thirty pounds. And one time I come out of a theater—one of them downtown theaters in Cleveland—and I looked in one of these side mirrors in the lobby as I was goin' out, and it looked like a short gorilla walkin' down there.

"That's the reason I'll never walk in a cafe. And I'll never accept a bus ticket. 'Cause I have to sit there and have people look at me all the time. And every time I look at them, they look away like this.

"But kids, they're different. I love kids. I love children. I don't know; I seem to attract 'em like a magnet. Every time I walk out of a small town, I have all these kids followin' me out. I feel like the Pied Piper of Hamelin. All these little girls, you know—about seven or eight years old—they all wanna take me home with 'em and mother me. 'Cause, you know, they don't think of me as an adult. Hell, I'm just a little man; I'm something unusual, and they're curious. If I saw me walkin' down the highway, I'd be a little curious myself. I'd say, 'What the hell *is* that?'

"But I'm on their level, and they ask me all kinds of questions. And I answer every question. Because, you know, any question that's asked by a child is very important to that child. So I answer.

"And of course I listen to 'em. I've been doin' that, I don't know, ever since I was young. All my relatives and all my friends, they always tell me their problems. And then I get out on the highway, tryin' to break away, and I run inta the same damn thing.

"First, they'll brag about their material possessions. Then when they see my reaction, they change over; they start tellin' me all their problems. And boy, do they have problems! Well, it kinda recharges my batteries, 'cause I know I'll never have as many problems as they have. Their number one problem is they gotta buy gas for their car. Ha ha. I don't have to do that. I can always get out and walk.

"But it's this so-called security thing they think they have. And then they have this cop-out of 'all *my responsibilities*. My home is not paid for . . . my children are still in college . . . my kids need dental work.' And this and that. And . . . 'I hate my job.'

"Ha. He's drivin' a Cadillac El Dorado, you know, or a Lincoln Continental. And they wanna change places, but at the same time, they don't wanna lose this so-called security they think they have with that paycheck comin' all the time. But they're afraid to take a chance, really, on something new. Me, if I wake up in the morning, I feel *very* secure—believe me! Man, it's another day! Let's see what's gonna happen!

"But the average person is afraid to take a chance, see? On something that's unknown. They keep holding onto their same patterns and living a life of utter frustration—*desperate* frustration, I think you call it. And always complaining about something that they're afraid to take a chance on.

"Of course, they're tryin' to elicit sympathy at the same time. And, you know, many people I meet, they give me the impression that the more miserable they are, the happier they are. They've got something to talk about; otherwise, their life is nothing. Ha ha.

"Actually, I'll tell you, Richard, I finally realized after fifteen years that what I'm doin' along the highway is runnin' a nonprofit counseling service. Jeez, I never get nothin' for anything. Just listen to their problems.

"I've ridden in Buicks and Cadillacs and with millionaires and in Lincoln Continentals—and once in Yuma, Arizona, I climbed into a Rolls Royce. I rode in a Rolls Royce, but I've never got a ride in a Chrysler yet. In fifteen years, no Chrysler has ever stopped. Chryslers are my anathema.

"One thing I won't do is get in the back of a truck. There's no protection back there. And then they're gonna let me off where they think is good for me—smack dab in the middle of town by a traffic light.

"They'll say, 'Oh, I've seen hitchhikers here before. They got rides.' But they didn't watch how long the hitchhikers were standin' there. Some of 'em were standin' there for seventeen weeks, tryin' to get a ride outta there. No—I won't take a ride in the back of a pickup. I used to, but not anymore.

"There are so many cars I won't get into. It's just the little things I know. I've learned, now, that if a car stops up ahead and just sits there and waits for me to walk up to it—I won't walk up to it. I'll stay right where I am, because I know that man—I've run into this many times, I've learned it the hard way—that if I get into that car, he's gonna take me to *his* destination. And I've also learned that no matter which direction I'm traveling—east, west, north or south—*nobody* ever lives on the other side of a town. They all live on this side of town or smack dab in the middle, and the driver will not go *one inch* past his destination. He'll leave me right in the middle of town or on this side of it.

"But if the car stops and the man backs up, then I know that there's hope for him, see. There's a pretty good chance I'll ride with him. And when a man stops, backs up, gets *out* of the car, and wants to help me with my backpack, I'll ride with him all day long.

"But things have changed. When I started out fifteen years ago, people were really thinking of each other. They were more compassionate, not as self-centered as they are now. Now, they don't like to become involved. They're all so wrapped up in their little world where nothin' rocks the boat, and they don't wanna change that.

"And then there's so many chiselers on the highways, hitchhiking. There's a lot of nice ones—I've met so many nice ones—but there's too many of the others, too. And now, they don't even talk to one another. And I know this past year, more and more are going back home again—where they belong—which is less competition for me. I'm kind of a selfish sonofagun anyway. I'd rather have the whole highway to myself.

"Well, I've got the shoulder. I just try to walk as far to the right as I can. My one crutch is always off the highway—I walk right on the edge of it. And if it's pretty level, I'll walk on the dirt rather than on the shoulder of the road.

"If the wind is blowing in my direction, every time a truck comes by I brace myself, just automatically. I hold onto my cap. That's why I don't wear any more Western hats—oh, *boy*! Every time a truck came by, I was chasin' my hat all over the state of Texas. Ha ha.

"You know, there's a lot of open spaces once you get west of Abilene, all the way to El Paso and all the way across into Arizona. In fact, from there to Abilene, halfway across to California, is nothing but desert. And I been up and down that thing so many times.

"I don't mind the desert. If the sun is out, I don't care if it's a hundred degrees or a hundred and fifteen degrees, as long as there's the slightest breeze blowing. If there's a breeze, it's nice; if it's stagnant, man, I just wanna get outta that part of the country.

"But I have to go down there for the winter. I'm not built tall enough to walk through any four-foot snowdrifts. Not without a periscope and a snorkel.

"I don't mind snow; I can brush snow off. What I don't appreciate is the rain—I can't brush that off. The rain will just deteriorate all these clothes, and they'll just rot away. I'll tell ya, with me, when something starts to fall apart, everything falls apart at the same time. I don't mess around. Everything falls apart at the same time.

"And if I run outta groceries, I run outta tobacco also, and I run outta water, and I run outta this, and I run outta that. All at the same time. Well, it gives me a sense of accomplishment. If I survive for the day, I say '*Hallelujah*!'

"It's an interesting way of life, not knowing what's gonna happen—that's what makes it so exciting. I can hobble anyplace, and for some reason—I don't care how weird or how far out a man is—when he sees me, there's always a little compassion. And I *listen* to that man. All I have to do is listen when he talks—and you know, sympathize.

"I've got that down to a fine art anyway. I've had a lot of practice. And I like people, in spite of themselves. And they sense it. I've met so many people—all kinds, from the roughest weirdos to the intellectuals. And I find that basically they're all the same; there's no difference between 'em.

"And then they accept me like a father image, which kinda hurts my feelings, 'cause I'm not that old. No—father isn't bad; it's when they call me *gramps* it really hurts my feelings.

"But I made up my mind years ago to live to be one hundred years old. Now I've only got 41 more to go. And I think on my hundredth birthday, I'm just gonna hike off inta the mountains and sit under a tree somewhere. I'll sit there and watch clouds. And after I'm dead, the coyotes can eat me. They'll take a bite outta me and they'll burp and they'll say, 'Oh boy, that Stanley was a good man! He was good for *something*!'"

Two Car Bob's
demise might have passed
unnoticed had it not been
for an obituary penned
by Harvard graduate
Arthur Kenneth Donoghue.

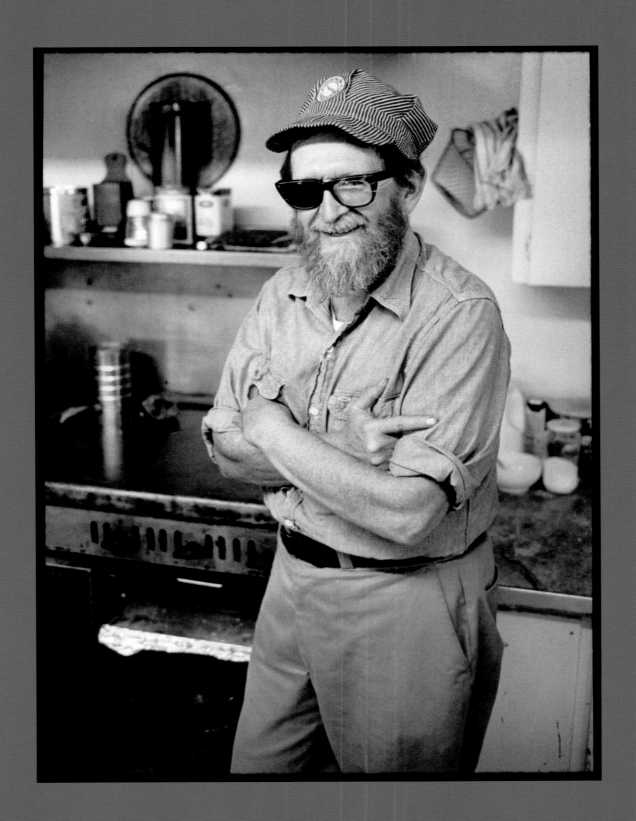

CHAPTER FIVE

Two Car Bob

Stanley Gurcze had occasionally gotten lucky in Nevada. Once, on the outskirts of Carson City, he'd been picked up by Governor Paul Laxalt, who had bought him a six-pack of beer and directed his chauffeur to drive Stan "wherever he wants to go." At a Las Vegas craps table one night, Stan had parlayed a fourteen dollar investment into $450, and a pretty young woman had followed him out the door. It's amazing what a difference money makes. Legs or no legs, people look up to you. But if you're down and out, your friends tend to drift away. And if you're dead, they drift even farther.

Theodor "Bob" Heist was both poor *and* dead, and so far removed from mainstream society that his body lay in state for five days before anyone even noticed. He was mourned only by his fiercely loyal mongrel dog, Taco, which had to be shot by a sheriff's deputy before the county coroner could get close enough to determine that the deceased had drunk himself to death.

Born in Germany and a veteran of the U.S. Army, Heist had lived in Wendover for five years. Yet no one in Wendover attended his funeral, which took place 120 miles away in Elko. To be sure, it wasn't much of a funeral—just a perfunctory graveside service underwritten by the Veteran's Administration. Probably no one would have taken notice of his passing, had not Arthur Kenneth Donoghue penned a brief obituary for the *Salt Flat News*.

Ken Donoghue was a native of Boston and a graduate of Harvard University. In the early 1970s, he'd been hired on as the food and wine editor of the *Salt Flat News*. Between infrequent assignments, Donoghue served as spiritual adviser and wine steward to Jim Smith, son of casino magnate William Smith.

Donoghue's "office" was a one-room shack perched atop a barren rock pile, shadeless except during the early morning hours when it fell underneath the shadow cast by the animated colossus Wendover Will. His furnishings consisted of books and wooden crates filled with the finest wines Jim Smith's money could buy. Because there was no wine cellar, the only way Kenneth could control quality was by rotating the stock. In other words, he drank it.

Whenever I was in town, I'd lend him a hand—and a hollow leg. Ken was an excellent host—well traveled, highly educated, and fluent in half a dozen languages. He had lived many years abroad, and was a good friend and frequent houseguest of the Irish writer J.P. Donleavy. I've heard it said that he was the inspiration for Donleavy's central character in *The Ginger Man*.

Ken Donoghue didn't gamble; however, he'd spent many an hour observing the action at Jim's Casino and had come to the conclusion that the object of the game is not winning but losing.

"I actually hear people bragging about their losses," he told me. "'Oh, what a *beating* I took last night,' they'll say. Or: 'Let me tell you, I got *killed* at the craps table.'"

"Sounds more like complaining than bragging to me," I said.

"No, it's bragging, trust me. And the worse the beating, the better they feel afterward. It's what people *expect* to happen; it's what they come out here for."

"How so?" I asked, wiping the dust from a bottle of Chateau Rothschild Bordeaux with my shirtsleeve.

"Well, just *listen* to them. They sit around the table all night chanting, 'Hit me . . . hit me again. Hit me *harder*!' Then the dealer will ask, 'How many do you want?' What he's saying is, 'How many *lashes* do you desire?'"

"Oh, that's just crazy," I said. "Most players don't say anything when they're at the table—they just point."

"Of course, they don't come right out and say what it is they want," answered Ken. "It's a repressed thing, this psychic need to be mugged. Tell me—why do you suppose they call the game *blackjack*?"

"They don't call it blackjack," I countered. "In Nevada, it's called twenty-one."

"Like I said, it's a repressed thing."

"I see."

Ken refilled my Styrofoam cup from a bottle of Chassagne-Montrachet 1945.

I passed out early that evening, coming to just as the first rays of dawn were breaking over the casino parking lot. I stepped out of my minivan onto asphalt that was littered with discarded beer cans, plastic cocktail glasses, swizzle sticks, and countless cigarette butts.

I decided to take a walk, making my way through the trailer park suburb known as Scobieville, then along the railroad tracks that separate Wendover's poor from her desperately poor. By and by I came upon the two junked cars that, until recently, had served as Bob Heist's home.

One was a 1949 Chevy, which Heist had adapted as a sitting room and library. The other, a 1953 Dodge, served as his bedroom. A heater fashioned from a fifty-gallon oil drum kept him warm in the winter. During the summer, he'd slept outdoors on a makeshift couch. Not exactly the Ritz, but as Kenneth Donoghue had pointed out in his obituary, Bob Heist *had* succeeded in achieving the dream of many an American in that he owned two cars.

Judging from the many magazines and books lying about, I surmised that "Two Car" Bob must have been an avid reader as well as an avid drinker. Except for the occasional trip to the post office or furtive shopping excursion to Rippetoe's General Store, Heist had avoided people. The only person he had ever spoken to at length was his nearest neighbor, Floyd Eaton, and it was Eaton to whom I now turned for further information.

"Well, he was . . . he was . . . well, I guess he was about five foot eleven inches tall," declared Eaton. "Weighed about a hunnert and eighty, a hunnert and ninety pounds. He was heavyset, and his first name wasn't Bob. His name was Theodor, but he went by the name of Bob all the time."

"So, then, it's still *another* case of someone living under an assumed name?"

"Uh huh."

Eaton told me he had chatted often with Two Car Bob because Bob's encampment happened to be next to an underground water pipe that carries culinary water to Wendover from Johnson Spring.

"There's a big valve there, and that's where I git all my water, right down there by the cars. Take my water jugs down there, climb in the hole, and fill 'em up. And most of the time, old Bob, he'd git down in there and fill 'em up fer me. And then he'd come down't the house a lotta times, set and talk to me."

"Did he ever tell you how he came to be homeless?" I asked.

"Well, he done it on purpose. He went out on the bum on purpose, yes sir."

"On purpose?"

"Yep. I imagine he'd been on the road fer years. He was a butcher by trade—had his own shop and ever'thang—a meat packin' outfit. But then his wife said she wanted a place in the country. So he bought a place in the country, got a little farm and started workin' it. Well, by the time he got ever'thang ready—got it workin' to where it would pay him back a little bit—why, then she wanted to move back to town."

"So she still wasn't happy?"

"No, *sir*!" Eaton whipped out his Zippo and kindled a fresh pipeload of Sir Walter Raleigh. His cheeks collapsed around the stem like a blacksmith's bellows. Then came an eruption of aromatic smoke. On the linoleum floor Tina stirred, wagged her tail, and panted as her master's hand gently massaged the nape of her neck.

"Nope, she *still* wasn't happy," Floyd resumed. "And by and by she divorced him and sued for alimony. She got ever'thang he owned."

Pant, pant, pant. Wag, wag, wag. Why can't a woman be more like a Border collie?

"And . . . he just made his mind up, said, 'Hell, there's one way t' fix her, right real good.' Says, 'I'll just go out on the bum and not work.' And he says, 'If I ain't *got* the money, she cain't *git* the money!'

"So that's what he done. He just went out on the goddamn bum t' keep from payin' his wife alimony."

So, from a certain perspective, I suppose it could be argued that Two Car Bob's demise wasn't the tragedy it appeared to be on the surface, but rather one man's triumph over the legal system. It all set me to wondering whether there might not be a Mrs. Eaton back home in Texas or Louisiana or Mississippi—wherever it was Floyd originally came from.

"Hell . . . *no*!" was his emphatic reply. "I never made that mistake. No, sir, that's one mistake I never did make.

"You see that little bronze holly wreath hangin' on the wall there? With that motto on it? Well, I found that sonofabitch up on the dump one day. It was layin' upside down, but I seen it was bronze, so I picked it up. I just stuck it in my hip pocket with some other junk I had—pieces of brass, copper, and stuff.

"When I got back to the house, I was gonna throw the sonofabitch in the junk bag. But then I seen it had writin' on it. I wiped the dust off, reached over and got my glasses, and put 'em on so I could see what it was."

"And . . . ?"

"Says, 'It don't matter how *successful* a man may be, there's always a woman standin' behind him tellin' him he's wrong.'

"So I got me a tack—a big, old roofin' nail—and I tacked it right up on the wall. And I says, 'That's where that sonofabitch is gonna stay.' I says, 'That's *jest right!*'"

I passed the remainder of our visit snapping pictures of Floyd and Tina—and, for the record, a close-up of the wall plaque bearing the words bold men in landfills live and die by. I was using a vintage 30-year-old Leica camera with a 5cm f/3.5 Elmar lens coupled to an optical close-focusing optical device—whimsically nicknamed "Nooky" by its German inventor, Oskar Barnack. As I focused on the plaque, Eaton looked on with interest.

"Wait a minute!" he exclaimed, as I was about to put the camera back in my gadget bag. "I've got somethin' I think you can use."

Eaton burrowed into his junk bag and withdrew a small, black Moroccan leather case with a brass zipper—just the thing, he declared, to contain the close-focusing optical device.

"Found it the other day up on the dump," he explained.

"Why, thank you, Floyd," I said. And I really meant it. For something that had come off a garbage dump, it was quite a nice little accessory.

Now, to my knowledge, no one who lives in Wendover owns a 30-year-old Leica camera. As for the Nooky, the only one I've ever seen is my own. A Moroccan leather Nooky carrying case? According to the dozens of collector's catalogs I've pored over, there is no such thing. Yet it accommodates my precious Nooky perfectly!

Later that evening, I took Floyd's gift out of my gadget bag for a closer look. Now I could see that there was something written on the case; I wiped away the dust and reached for my reading glasses. The inscription read:

LEICA
E. Leitz
Wetzlar, Germany

"When I think of expiring,

I start perspiring."

— Carl Hayden

There he was laid to rest along with his favorite fishing rod, reel, and line.

"A nonjoiner, never a community activist," Hayden concluded, "Mr. Spence went fishing almost daily. Mostly to Little Salmon River and Shoshone Creek because of their nearness, but he took longer trips on his days off work. At the time of his death, he was leading in the smallmouth bass division of Cactus Pete's $1800 fishing contest."

Inserting a plug for his employer's fishing contest into the middle of an obituary is more than just a prime example of Hayden's unwavering commitment to his calling as casino publicist. That Roy Spence should be suddenly and unexpectedly reeled in while leading in the smallmouth bass division of a fishing tournament is also a telling commentary on the human condition. Are we the fishermen, or are we the fish? *That* is the question!

With three casinos, three motels, two gas stations, two gift shops and one traffic light, Jackpot today thrives as never before. On weekends the aerodrome-sized parking lots are jam-packed with motor homes bearing license plates from all over the country. Hotel rooms are booked solid months in advance, and all seats are sold out for Saturday night's upcoming concert in the Gala Room, where Glen Campbell will sing "By The Time I Get To Phoenix," "Easy On My Mind," and other timeless anthems of noncommitment before an audience consisting of gray-haired couples who've been together, on average, fifty years.

The Carl Hayden-Cactus Pete marriage endured almost twenty years, until August 11, 1992—the day Carl passed away just one day after meeting his final deadline. His last newsletter contained no news whatsoever—only a lengthy tribute to the hardy barrel cactus, which miraculously grows in the rockiest of soils with but two drops of rain a year. It ended thus:

Let there be light
Part of each night
So there is no fright
Good night.

* * *

Even as Carl Hayden labored tirelessly to promote the gaming industry, Tom Clay was working just as hard to abolish it. In Clay's view, gaming wasn't even an industry; it was an organized crime that had turned Nevada into "a black spot on the face of the nation."

Otherwise, the two men had a lot in common. Like Carl, Tom lived alone and was financially secure. Both men went to work every day, and both were writers. Both were senior citizens—albeit at age 96, Tom Clay no longer likened himself to a sex act.

Clay also lived alongside Highway 93—about three hundred miles down the road from Jackpot, just beyond the city limits of Panaca in Lincoln County. Lincoln County was named in honor of the 16th President, who in 1864 had sponsored Nevada's admission into the Union because the North desperately needed the territory's silver and gold to finance its war against the Confederacy.

Except for a handful of stately buildings erected back in those halcyon days, Lincoln County's architecture consists mostly of ramshackle cabins and house trailers. The squalor is magnified when one compares Lincoln County with booming Clark County to the south, and one needn't hold an MBA from Harvard to figure out why: whereas Clark County has a hundred casinos, Lincoln County doesn't have even one.

What Lincoln County does have is a weekly newspaper, the *Lincoln County Record*, which, during Tom Clay's tenure as editor and publisher, was unlike any other publication in the state. Scrolled in bold type across the top of the front page of each issue was the same banner headline:

INTELLIGENCE, PATRIOTISM, CHRISTIANITY, AND A FIRM RELIANCE ON HIM WHO HAS NEVER YET FORSAKEN THIS FAVORED LAND, ARE STILL COMPETENT TO ADJUST IN THE BEST WAY, ALL OUR PRESENT DIFFICULTY.

The statement was attributed to Abraham Lincoln, and sounds like something Abe might have written during the dark days of the Civil War. Was a new civil war raging in Lincoln County?

I had heard a lot about Tom and thus was apprehensive about meeting him face to face. In order to fortify myself, I'd stopped at the general store in Panaca and bought a six-pack of beer, several sticks of pepperoni, and an assortment of potted meat products. I also picked up a current issue of the *Lincoln County Record*, which, according to the masthead, had been established way back in 1870. The issue in my hands was number 22 of volume 106. On the front page, just below the Abraham Lincoln quote, was a birth announcement: a baby boy born to Billy and Janice Smith of Pioche. There was also one obituary, that of longtime resident Sibyl Pennington Amante, who had requested no services and no flowers. Then there was an article about Stanley E. Deal, formerly employed as a physician at the Lincoln County Hospital in Caliente. Dr. Deal had been tried and found guilty of dealing narcotics—a felony for which he'd been sentenced to serve ten years in the Nevada State Penitentiary.

Newswise, that was it. The remainder of the newspaper consisted of densely packed columns of print, outwardly similar to a legal notice:

The editor has before him the minutes of the County Commissioners Meeting of June 20, 1977, which are as long as the longest day of the

year on which they met. The minutes record generally the routine actions the Commissioners are required to attend, but the big issue of the new whorehouse was presented not by its representatives, but by an attorney representing a sister whorehouse, which doesn't want its sister in competition. The complaint of the sister intruding was set out in the *Record's* last issue and took up a hell of a lot of space . . .

It was hard to tell exactly where the local news ended and the editorial page began, so similar was the tone. Letters to the editor all rang vaguely familiar as well, each beginning with the same folksy salutation. To wit:

Folks! I've just had a darn good lecture.

The people of Lincoln County want whorehouses, why are you against them? When the commissioners enacted ordinances against whoring, it was against the will of the people.

At one time, the people of the United States wanted Negro slavery and they had slaves. A few people, among whom was Lincoln, said it is not common sense and therefore wrong. Common sense embraces morals and common sense abolished Negro slavery. Common sense will abolish the legality of gambling or I am wrong in the estimate of the power of common sense: the zenith of God's creation.

I asked the woman behind the counter where I might find the publisher of the *Lincoln County Record*.

"Who . . . *him*?!" You would have thought I'd just asked where I could get my copy of *Mein Kampf* autographed.

She explained there was no longer a newspaper office in Panaca. I was told to continue south on Highway 93 until I came to the 1001 Ranch. "That's . . . *him*."

The 1001 was an attractive spread, with a barn, tack sheds, and stables spread out behind a modest white ranch house. Inside the house, I was greeted by the *Record*'s sole remaining employee—a young woman by the name of Carolyn Thompson.

"I'm here to interview Thomas Clay," I announced.

"You want to talk to *him*?!"

Carolyn pointed me in the direction of a white, cinder block bunker out back. She didn't offer to accompany me.

Posted on the door of the bunker was a sign. It read: **"Everything Is Just Fine."**

Tom Clay didn't get up when I knocked—just beckoned me in a gruff voice to come in. His office was lined from floor to ceiling with books, none of which were on the current best-seller list. Mostly they were reference books and legal tomes, interspersed with framed mottos and patriotic credos. I spotted the name Elbert Hubbard.

Clay's desktop was completely buried under a mound of papers, books, and notepads. On top of the pile was balanced a star-spangled coffee mug and a Webster's dictionary. There was also an ashtray heaped high with cigarette butts.

Clay wore an olive green work shirt and matching gabardine pants, dark socks, and a pair of white Converse high top basketball sneakers. He ordered me to sit down and state my business. As I did so, he took a noisy gulp from his star-spangled coffee mug and a deep drag from a Chesterfield cigarette.

"Okay, shoot the works and I won't break in on ya," he declared. "You ask the questions, and you'll find out I'm the biggest goddamn liar in Lincoln County."

I began by asking if, in the interest of health, he'd ever considered giving up smoking—or at least cutting back. Clay answered that he'd once tried switching to filter-tipped cigarettes, but found "it was like sucking a nipple through a nightgown."

61

"I've smoked 'em for sixty years, and if you'll notice, I damn near chain smoke," he said. "I've had remarkable health, but that's no brief for smoking cigarettes. I think the surgeon general is right: they are hazardous. But the big thing is, I haven't guts enough to quit. God, I've quit a million times, but I lack guts."

I learned that Tom had been born on the plains of Nebraska on October 2, 1882. He had started grade school in Kansas and graduated from the University of Southern California in 1910. Following a stint in the U.S. Army during World War I, he'd practiced civil law for thirty years in Riverside, California.

Clay also raised horses in California from 1929 until 1962, the year he'd retired from law and moved his herd of prize-winning Appaloosas to the wide open spaces of southern Nevada.

"I built everything that's here," he declared. "This was all sagebrush when I came here. I owned everything between here and Caliente, practically—but you know, by God, a fella has to deal with realities. I'd bought this paper, I had this ranch, and I got to thinking one night it's a lot to handle.

"So, I have a very close friend that I've known for many years who owns a truck line—a big outfit, from Phoenix to Seattle. When I first met him he had two trucks, and when he sold out five or six years ago, he had 375 trucks and trailers. All paid for.

"I knew he wanted to get a ranch, so I called him on the phone one night and I said, 'Well, you're gonna take over my ranch. When can you be here?'

"He said, 'I'll be there at ten-thirty in the morning.' He had his own plane, and he came, and he sat down in that chair—right where you are. And in less than twenty minutes, he and I did a deal. Of damn near a million dollars—all based on my estimate of his character, and his estimate of mine."

Not everyone who'd sat in my chair had passed Tom Clay's character test. Carl Hayden had told me about a horse trader who had purchased several head of stock from the 1001. A price had

been agreed upon and the animals had already been loaded onto a transport truck when the buyer let drop a remark suggesting that Clay had got the better of him in the deal. Tom promptly ordered his men to unload the horses, handed the trader his money back, and booted him off his property.

People who worked for Clay soon learned to keep their opinions to themselves. A former employee of the newspaper told me that one day after returning home from work, he'd picked up a sledge hammer and beaten the family Corvair into a pulp. "It was either the car or Mr. Clay," he explained.

Since Tom Clay had taken over the newspaper, circulation had dropped from 1500 to 250, and by Carolyn Thompson's estimate, there weren't more than five citizens in Lincoln County who could speak well of her boss. "People get tired of being preached at all the time," she told me.

But such criticism didn't seem to faze Tom Clay, who figured the fifty grand he'd sunk into the venture was a reasonable price to command such a bully pulpit.

"Here's a great state," he declared, "with a wealth of natural resources. All they need is developing, to make wealth for people—but instead of doing that, we just live as parasites off of people we can get to come here and take away their money. We live off *unthinking* people. It's that thing in all of us—we want to get something for nothing. Like a casino down there in Vegas has got a sign up: "Come in and double your paycheck." Well, if people could *do* that, where in the hell would the casino be? P.T. Barnum said there's a fool born every minute, but he wasn't acquainted with Nevada, I don't think. I think there's *two*."

Clay shuffled through the pile of papers on his desk and pulled out a document I immediately recognized as the *Donoghue Letter*, a monthly gaming industry newsletter published by erstwhile Wendover sommelier Kenneth Donoghue. Working out of a post office box in Carson City, Ken was billing subscribers five dollars per four-page issue. Unlike the *Lincoln County Record*, *his* circulation was growing.

Tom read aloud a passage from the newsletter that he'd underlined in shaky ballpoint: "Once considered a 'shady business' because of its allegedly unsavory underworld associations, gaming is now considered a respectable business . . . "

Clay cast the newsletter aside, took a gulp of coffee, and lit up a fresh Chesterfield. "What the hell kind of a state can you have," he thundered, "when everything hinges on living off the weaknesses of man?"

Playing the devil's advocate, I pointed out that farming and ranching are precarious enterprises. The precious metal market is volatile as well, and ore veins have a tendency to pinch out. But *human weaknesses*! Seems to me the state of Nevada has tapped into an inexhaustible resource.

"But it's *Mammon*!" countered Tom. "What I mean is, they're putting bread and butter ahead of morals. A man doesn't live by bread alone. He's gotta have *some* bread, but there's another part of him that's just as big, that's gotta be nurtured also. If he's a *man*."

But didn't it trouble him, I wondered, that probably no more than five people in the entire county agreed with his position?

"No," he answered emphatically. "I don't think you can measure things by their popularity. Jesus wasn't very popular. Lincoln had to sneak into Washington to keep from being assassinated. I don't think Truman was appreciated so much when he was president, but now when we look back on it, he's going down as one of our great presidents. And the big thing he had was *guts*. And I say this: I'm an egotist; I like pats on the back. But the pats that really mean anything is when I can pat myself on the back, if you get what I mean."

Tom Clay went on to say he envisioned a day when America would become a nation grounded on principle and governed by men and women of high moral character. Ours would become a second Age of Enlightenment, a return to the days of Tom Jefferson and Tom Paine, when "great ideas were in the air."

He concluded the interview by asking *me* a question: had I come because I was interested in what he had to say? Or was I there only—as he phrased it—"because I'm a unique antique?"

Truthfully—because I knew he wouldn't settle for anything less—I confessed that I was probably more interested in the medium than the message. I said I found it amazing that a man who had become eligible to receive Social Security thirty years earlier would still be working a seven-day week. I was curious why Tom, who could clearly afford it, hadn't bought himself a motor home and launched himself upon that geriatric road to romance that runs right past his house?

"It's anathema to me, retirement," Tom growled, lighting up still another Chesterfield. "When a man retires and just fishes and so forth and so on, he's of no goddamn use. He's just eating up our substance, living off the beans, so to speak. And in a while, he gets pretty goddamn bored himself."

I sensed that Tom was fast growing weary of my company. After all, he had a deadline to meet, and already I'd taken up half an hour of his precious time. So I thanked him for the interview and offered to show myself to the door. Tom waved goodbye without getting up and turned back to the paragraph he'd been working on before the interruption.

I spent the remainder of a hot summer afternoon canvassing Lincoln County in search of the alleged five citizens willing to speak well of Tom Clay, but couldn't find even one. Instead, all I found were a lot of run-down houses, a brothel under construction, and a number of busted-up automobiles that looked as if some crazy person had taken a sledgehammer to them.

"I'll tell ya,
I'm happy up here.
When you've been around
the public for a while,
you get tired of it."

— Ray Walker

CHAPTER SEVEN

Lonely, Lonelier, Loneliest

In July 1986, *LIFE* magazine named the stretch of U.S. Highway 50 that spans western Utah and central Nevada the loneliest road in the country. "It's totally empty," declared a spokesman for the American Automobile Association. "There are no points of interest. We don't recommend it. We warn all motorists not to drive there unless they're confident of their survival skills."

My introduction to the nation's loneliest highway came in November 1957. At the time I was one of a dozen Explorer Scouts from Utah bound for Stead Air Force Base near Reno, where we were scheduled to undergo a week of paramilitary survival training at a forest camp high in the Sierra Nevada mountains.

More rigorous than survival camp, however, was the bus ride across the Great Basin. Our vintage school bus had no heater, few operative gauges, a dodgy drive train, and a rapidly failing engine. As we were climbing Connors Pass in the Schell Creek Range, the shift lever came loose in the driver's hand. The passengers jumped out and eased the vehicle back down the grade to Major's Place.

By the time we pulled into Ely, several windows had fallen out, including the one I was seated next to. Descending Pony Canyon into Austin, the brakes failed, and for the second time that day, we were obliged to bail out. It seemed as though I had jumped backward in time as well. Austin, with its well-worn wooden boardwalks, sagging roofs, and weathered clapboard storefronts was straight out of a dime novel—the quintessential Western frontier town. Then and there, I vowed that, should I be fortunate enough to survive the survival trip, I'd one day return to The Land That Time Forgot.

Exactly ten years later, I found myself traveling west on Highway 50 again, this time curled in a fetal position in the nonexistent back seat of Ron Crouch's Austin-Healy convertible. Rain was falling, but Ron couldn't put the top up. The top, he confessed, had taken flight in a crosswind on a previous trip.

Ron was a rarity, one of the West Desert's few native sons. He'd grown up in the remote Snake Valley settlement of Eskdale, a religious commune founded in the 1940s by a visionary chiropractor named Glendenning. Dr. Glendenning had chosen the site because land in Snake Valley was cheap and as far removed from urban distractions as any piece of real estate outside of Antarctica could possibly be.

A hundred miles west of Delta, Ron steered the Healy off the pavement and onto a rutted dirt lane bordered by giant sagebrush plants and anthills the size of foothills. Hailstones battered our bared heads, thunder rolled, lightning bolts crackled and sizzled all around us.

Presently we arrived at a compound of white frame cabins clustered about a church and school. From inside the school came strains of Mozart; we'd arrived just in time to enjoy a matinee performance by the Eskdale Symphony Orchestra!

Since that day, I've traversed the nation's loneliest road many times. Each time I've experienced loneliness, compounded by culture shock. Until recently, for example, there wasn't a single restaurant franchise or chain affiliated motel to be found between Delta, Utah, and Fallon, Nevada—a distance of over 400 miles!

The gaudy gaming emporia that brighten the skylines of so many Nevada towns are nowhere to be found in central Nevada. Between the Hotel Nevada in Ely and the Nugget in Fallon you won't find a blackjack table, craps table, or roulette wheel.

Here and there you *might* encounter a slot machine—but just as casinos are said to position their loosest machines near the entrances, the stingiest ones reside in the Silver State's dark interior. The story is told of a burglar who broke into a Eureka bar and made off with a one-armed bandit. Months later, a prospector in Railroad Valley stumbled upon the thief's skeletal remains, his bony fingers still clutching the handle of the miserly machine—which in captivity had gained weight.

U.S. 50 threads its way through faded hamlets that, in times past, were Nevada's major cities. The loneliest road itself was once a busy thoroughfare. The Pony Express and Overland Stage routes both crossed central Nevada, as did the nation's first transcontinental road, the Lincoln Highway. However, with the completion of U.S. 40, traffic patterns changed. Northern outposts grew while central Nevada towns shrank. Meantime, those few hardy denizens who stayed put—like the land after the waters of Lake Bonneville receded—have grown ever saltier and crustier.

* * *

If such a thing as prosperity has visited Lonely Land in recent years, then Ely is where it happened. Situated between the open pit copper mines at Ruth and the smelter town of McGill, Ely citizens can at least *remember* what a thriving economy feels like. By the time I came upon the scene, however, Kennecott Copper was in the process of shutting down and pulling out. The unemployment rate had soared to Depression era levels and every merchant in town was feeling the pinch, including the owner and operator of the Ely Pastry Shop, Maria "Mom" Pavlakis.

For half a century Mom Pavlakis' bakery had been a fixture on the west end of Aultman Street. There she had nursed her emphysemic husband for years until his death. On her own, she'd raised four sons and two daughters and put all six through college. It was rumored that she was sending money back to Greece to support relatives she'd never met, including a nephew she was helping put through medical school. "A great woman," one of her regular customers told me. "Everyone in town just loves her."

The afternoon I walked into her shop, Maria made it clear she had neither the time nor patience to entertain nosy newspaper reporters.

"I don't mind the work," she explained. "24 hours a day, I don't mind—I swear to God, honey, I no mind to work. But I no lika company. I lika my customens, I lika my home, I lika my family, I lika my work, I lika my dog. But I no like *nobody* else."

I reintroduced myself and restated my intentions. I assured her I hadn't come to pry into her personal affairs. What I wanted was to write an upbeat, heartwarming feature story. A human interest piece. But Mom Pavlakis would have no part of it.

"No me," she insisted. "I don't lika to waste my time for nobody. You understand now? So be good boy . . ."

Clearly, Mom Pavlakis was no publicity hound. But since she hadn't yet turned loose her German shepherd Spicer, I stood my ground. I decided to buy a sweet roll and half a dozen doughnuts—a

transaction I hoped might elevate me from the lowly status of nosy reporter to "good customen."

"Well," I continued as she went about filling my order, "let's just say I'm curious. I couldn't help noticing, for instance, that you have an autographed picture of Wayne Newton on the wall. Is he a friend of yours?"

"Wayne Newt?" Maria made a face. "Yeah, he send that. I haven lotta pictures. People do that for me—too many, honey. I swear to God, I be honest with you, I don't give a shit."

There were other celebrity photographs on the wall, including an 8" x 10" glossy signed by the governor of Nevada. Remembering that former first lady Pat Nixon was an Ely native, I asked Maria if she kept in touch with the White House.

"Me? Get mixed up with the dirty sonofabitches? No *way!*"

"Why not?"

"Never mix up with a politician or nothing'. Pat me, I pat you—no way! I no lika that. Senators, congressmens, govenments, supreme court judges, and what's his name, attorney general— what d'ya call that man? None of 'em worth ten cents, all of 'em for himselfs. *Everybody* for himselfs!"

"Ah, but . . . " I chewed slowly but my mind was racing. How best to tell the Mom Pavlakis story? In my head I was roughing out a storyline: displaced Old World immigrant comes to America, works hard, makes good in the Land of Opportunity. But Maria's train of thought apparently ran in the opposite direction.

"I come here 18-year-old girl," she declared. "Me raise and born in Turkey, but I'm Orthodox Greek. Our people, honey, they got plenty to eat. My father—export man! He ship a lotta stuff to world. His brother is a doctor and the other one a lawyer. You understand? My father a big export man—only one in Turkey. Beeg business, honey! So I no eatin' the garbage! I no *come* from garbage!

"But then Turkeys and Greeks got in a fight. I went to Greece, I stay there seven years. Me stay in Greece country in a small village. My father die heart attack. My mother die. I gotta one brother workin' Athens. And my brother, he tol' me, 'Maria, you haf to go to America. You be good to go there and help the rest of the family.'

"I say, 'How you lika to send me to America? I no gotta father, mother, brother, sister there. Alone and stranger, no language?'

"He say, 'You go be *rich*!'

"I say, 'I no lika to go.'

"He say, 'You haf to. Okay?'

"I say, 'No, no . . . '

"So my brother, *hit* me.

"So—what could I do? Couldn't do nothin', you know? Got no home, no folks, no land, no nothin'. Gotta do somethin' for a living, right? So I come.

"I tol' my brother, I say, 'You no go see me no more. Soon as I go inside the boat, you no go see me no more!' And then I never wrote my brother. 48 years—no way!"

"Because he hit you?" I asked.

"No. Because he send me to America!"

"But America . . . it's the Land of Opportunity."

"No, no, no, no. *No!* Why send *me* over? I'm no old, I'm no ugly, I'm no dummy. I'm no *crazy!* This kinda people come to America. All the dummies come to America, and everybody crazy in this country. Itsa *true*, honey!"

Our conversation was interrupted when a boy, about twelve years of age, entered the pastry shop, laid fifty cents on the counter, and asked for two sweet rolls. Maria grinned toothlessly and set about filling the young man's order.

On his way out, the boy paused to examine the contents of his paper sack. "Hey!" he exclaimed. "You gave me *three*."

"That's all right," Maria whispered. "I give it you. *Keep quiet!*"

From behind the front window of her pastry shop, Maria Pavlakis watched until her young customer had disappeared from sight.

"A lotta nice kids, honey," she sighed. "You know somethin'? I be honest with you—the kids, all of 'em, nice. All the kids is good in the world—but their *folks*, honey . . .

"Lotta people, marry people, lika to split up, come here to listen to me. I say, 'Listen, honey, whatcha doin' yesterday, forgit it. Let's go start a new life today. And be together, because you gotta children. The children are suffering.'"

"So you also do marriage counseling on the side?"

"Oh, yeah. A lot of 'em come here—a lot of 'em. A lotta people listen, because I'm straight. I'm strictly old fashioned kinda Mom, honey. Me lika to be honest—but now, people is no honestly with me. A lot of 'em jealous and mean. Two womens, I tell *stay way* from me. I don't want 'em close to me, honey, no. I no want 'em. I can't stand dirty people.

"The womens, honey—the first thing, they never had a good home. And the second thing, they think they gotta the pussy, they think they're God. The men marry, they give 'em right away, give 'em everything in the world. That goddamn pussy maka the mens *crazy*! You *see*? I'm right or I'm wrong?"

I had to admit that, yes, Maria's observation wasn't only painfully blunt but also reasonably accurate. At the same time, I couldn't help wondering where the girls who work at Ely's three brothels go whenever they get a hankering for a sweet roll?

It was almost closing time, and the late afternoon sun cast long shadows across the mostly vacant storefronts of downtown Ely. Maria Pavlakis, whose workday had started well before dawn, would be retiring about the same time the ladies at the Green Lantern would be rolling out of—and then back into—bed. Happy hour was fast approaching, but Maria Pavlakis, who'd never gambled nor tasted liquor in her entire life, wouldn't be a part of it.

No, she'd be in her own bed fast asleep, dreaming of what might have been, if *only* the Greeks and Turks had been able to get along.

As I walked away, I looked back to see her standing on the sidewalk in front of her bakery, her faithful German shepherd Spicer at her side. Maria was tossing handfuls of bread crumbs into the middle of Aultman Street. "Here, babies!" she cried. And suddenly the air was aflutter with birds. Every pigeon in White Pine County, evidently, ate at Mom's.

"Don't forget, my boy!" she shouted after me. "Don't forget! Everybody for *himselfs*!"

* * *

As the name suggests, Eureka was once the site of a big ore strike—primarily silver and lead. At the peak of the 1870s boom, the smokestacks of ten smelters darkened the sky, while tailing piles oozed arsenic into the soil and groundwater. Home to 9,000 souls, the so-called "Pittsburg of the West" was Nevada's second largest city.

A hundred years later, Eureka was all but a ghost town. The population had dwindled to just 350 citizens living among ruins, encircled by graveyards. Nearly every commercial building along Main Street was boarded up, and in each doorway lay a comatose dog. Other canines lounged in the middle of the road, indifferent to traffic. To me, it looked as if the dogs had taken over completely, and I was in town quite a while before I finally ran across a human being: a sprightly gentleman who introduced himself as Jack Killinger.

Killinger ran a rock shop on the ground floor of the historic Eureka Opera House. He wore a dark blue, well-worn suit and spoke in a precise, genteel manner. My impression was that he had emerged from another era. Had Killinger been around during

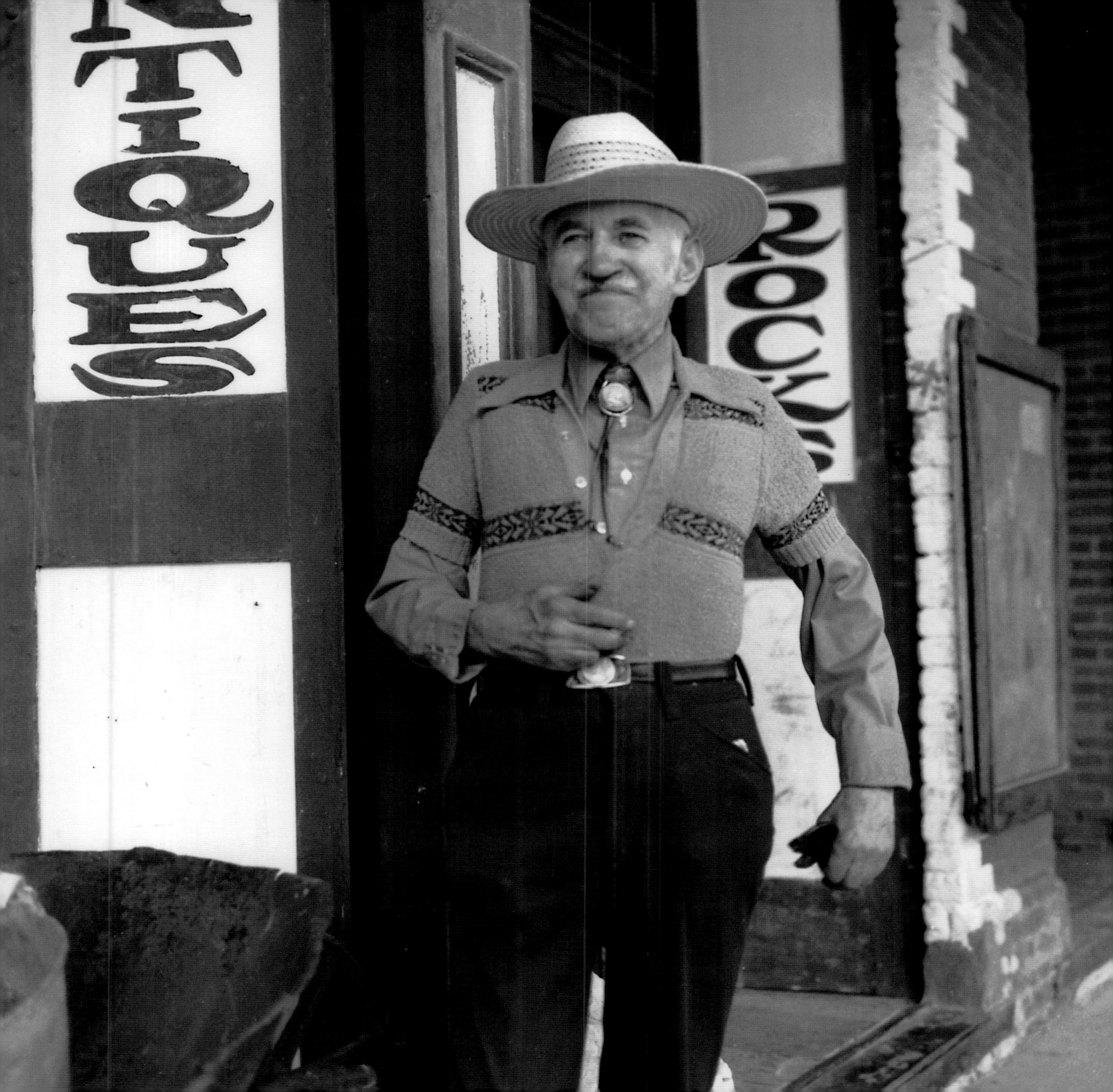
TIQUES
ROCKS

Eureka's heyday, most likely he would have occupied a prominent place in the community. He'd be a judge or perhaps the mayor.

Killinger's rock shop was a musty cavern stuffed floor to ceiling with curios, antique bottles, cheap costume jewelry, and fossil and mineral specimens that ran the gamut from semi-precious to worthless country rock. Out front was parked a wheelbarrow filled with the latter, topped with a sign: **"Free Samples."**

There were no customers in sight, and Jack seemed pleased to have someone other than himself to talk to for a change.

"I very seldom stay anywhere as long as I've stayed here," he confessed. "And I haven't been here all the time since I first came, because there was at least one year that I was mining turquoise near Austin."

In 1963, Jack had located a couple of claims in the nearby hills, but they hadn't panned out. It was typical of the way things had gone since the day he'd come into the world on the ninth of August, 1900. His father, he recalled, was a mining engineer who had worked in Pennsylvania, Nevada, California, and Lewiston, Idaho.

"He also went over to Mongolia, and he was in France on one occasion."

In the late 1880s, the senior Killinger went north to Alaska, but somehow managed to miss out on the Yukon gold rush. ("He was coming down Chilkoot Pass as the others were going up.")

When Jack was five years of age, his father ran off to Mexico and was never heard from again. Raised by his mother and a sister, Jack left home early and drifted from one place to another, living "very briefly in New Hampshire, a few years in New York, the best part of a year in New Jersey. I've lived in Philadelphia, and I also lived a very short time in North Carolina. And in California I lived in Berkeley and Sausalito and San Rafael and Redding, and I worked in a mine in Mariposa. I worked in San Diego for a while, during the Second World War in the Ryan Aircraft Company.

"I also had, at one time, a wholesale fur business. And another time I manufactured perfume. I got into that just at the wrong time, the worse possible time—1929. When the crash came, why, that really fixed me up."

Down but not out, Jack embarked on a career as an exterminator in Petaluma, where he became widely known as Jack the Ant Killer.

"But I got out of the pest control business because I accidentally poisoned myself with chlordane. And for about, oh, three, four, five years, I was absolutely unable to work. I'd get out of bed in the morning, and I'd be so full of ambition and energy and ready to go. And I wouldn't be two minutes out of the house until I was ready to go back to bed.

"I came very close to losing my life over it, I think. But I was fortunate. I went to half a dozen doctors, and none of 'em could do me any good. And I finally got the chlorine out of my system by taking some of these little tablets that they put into aquariums for tropical fish to take the chlorine out of the water. It took three years, but I finally got the chlorine out of my system."

Rejuvenated and dechlorinated, Jack resettled in Lake Tahoe, where he built a hotel and ran it for three years before selling out "for a very tiny profit." He hung around Tahoe for another year, giving private bridge lessons, then opened a secondhand store in Reno. After three months, the landlord ordered him to move on.

"So I gave that up and put the stuff in storage, and I went to Hawthorne, Nevada. And I stayed there as a watchman at the mill at Kinkead. The mill belongs to Captain Hal Hollaway. Hollaway was a United Airlines captain. He had a small airline that ran from L.A. to Avalon, and he gave United his franchise and became one of their first captains. Made a lot of money from the stock. Had a pension, a pension from Ethiopia. Was the founder of Ethiopian National Airlines, and I believe at the present he's mining silver somewhere a little bit east of Hawthorne, out of Mina, I think. A small mine . . . "

As Killinger's convoluted life story unfolded, it occurred to me that no two events are unrelated—that if only we could stand back far enough, we'd be able to see the connection between a hole in the ground in Nevada and an airline in Ethiopia. And we'd understand why, were there no such thing as tropical fish, people in Lake Tahoe wouldn't know how to play bridge. Connections, as James Burke might say.

Somehow I wasn't surprised to learn that Jack Killinger was also a writer. Under the pen name "Hugo" he had penned a weekly humor column for the *Eureka Miner*, an upstart local newspaper that had gone belly-up shortly after taking Killinger on as a correspondent. Jack led me to a dusty filing cabinet in the back of his store and pulled out a handful of his favorite essays. Subjects ranged from a tip on how to use a kangaroo to measure the altitude of airplanes, to a pseudoscientific treatise showing how the woodpecker evolved from the platypus. The columns were all typed on recycled stationery; the back side of each page bore this letterhead:

**Air Force Ballistic Missile
Division Headquarters Air Research
and Development Command
United States Air Force**

We ventured deeper into the bowels of the old opera house, whose cornerstone had been laid in 1879. The structure was originally intended to be a labor union hall, but then the union had gone broke and had been forced to sell the property before the hall was completed. So it became instead the Eureka Opera House, which was later converted into a combination dance hall and movie theater. Many years had passed, however, since the last picture show.

As I stood on the horseshoe-shaped balcony, looking down upon the frayed curtains, the rows of velvet upholstered seats, the dusty stage upon which the "Swedish Nightingale" Jenny Lind had once performed, I understood how the archeologist Howard Carter must have felt, beholding the tomb of Tutankhamen.

Jack spoke of other buried treasures, including a network of underground tunnels through which children used to make their way to school when the snow was too deep to plow. In Prohibition days, bootleggers used the tunnels to scuttle back and forth between still and bar, and during the Cold War, one of the tunnels had been designated a civil defense shelter.

Digging the tunnels had been easy, thanks to an abundance of skilled miners, muckers, and drillers. Lords of the underground, they had constituted a proud fraternity whose members had long since gone to graveyards. All, that is, except one.

* * *

It was Jack Killinger who introduced me to his neighbor Louis Gibellini, although I'd heard the name before in connection with the annual Nevada state hard rock drilling contest. At the 1970 state championship drill-off in Gabbs, Gibellini had shocked the drilling community by hammering a hole 3/4 of an inch in diameter and 11 and 9/32 inches deep into a block of sierra white granite in ten minutes flat. At the time he established the Nevada state single jack drilling record Louis Gibellini was 63 years old.

Louis was now in his early seventies, but still competing and frequently winning in spite of mounting health problems, including a recent bout with prostate cancer. He lived in a modest house at the north end of Eureka behind a seldom-open saloon he owned. Louie's Lounge was just a hobby for the proprietor, who earned a handsome living selling and reselling options on a vanadium claim to various large mining outfits.

Louis was frequently on the road, driving as far as Reno to get his hair cut, then to Sparks to visit his daughter and grandchildren. Then it was back to Reno for an evening of gambling, drinking, dancing, and carousing. Come morning, it was off to the hospital in Reno to undergo his scheduled radiation treatment.

"From past experience," observed Jack Killinger, "I would expect him to arrive about two or three in the morning. He sleeps very short hours at night and is usually out for his first cup of coffee around five A.M."

It wasn't hard to figure out which house was Gibillini's. A four-pound hammer and steel bits of various lengths lay near his doorway, and all the rocks around resembled Swiss cheese. The champion's gymnasium.

For all his medical problems, Louis Gibellini looked to be in excellent shape. His vigor was especially remarkable in light of the fact that drilling holes to accommodate dynamite charges ranks as one of the world's most dangerous occupations. In the first place, you're working underground. Second, you're messing with explosives. Worst of all, you're inhaling pulverized rock dust day in and day out, which lodges in the bronchial passages and over time results in a slow, painful suffocation known as pneumoconiosis. Rock splinters in the eyeballs; smashed fingers; busted-up hands; lungs filled with sulphurous, arsenical, metallic particles; a wooden headboard in the graveyard with your name on it—such was the lot of your typical steel-driving man in early Nevada.

"At my age," Gibellini laughed, "people say I should be *under* the rock, not over it."

Born in the mining camp of Prospect, a "subdivision" of Eureka, Louis had gone to work as a driller at the tender age of twelve. "We done it year in and year out; you hammered all day, all angles, this way, that way. I worked with guys, they made four of me, but I always kept up my end."

With the advent of the pneumatic drilling machine, human jackhammers like Louis soon found their skills were no longer in demand—except at Fourth of July celebrations featuring mining-related sporting events such as mucking, slag racing, single jack (one man) and double jack (two man) hard rock drilling.

Louis specialized in single jack, a category he'd dominated for several years until just recently, when he'd started coming in second to Fred Andreason of Virginia City. Louis had several theories as to why he'd lost to Andreason, none of which conceded any credit whatsoever to his upstart rival.

"I *never* was beaten excepting this last three years," he declared. "But when your steel starts fitchering, you're through. Last year I didn't do anything. My steel stuck from the beginning and I had a three-cornered hole. I was so loused up it was out of this world."

"What about Andreason?" I asked. "He's a lot younger than you are. Is it possible he's also stronger?"

"He doesn't hit as hard as I hit. He hits just like this." (Louis made a dainty motion with his wrist, like a shoemaker driving tacks.) "But I use my shoulder; I hit a harder blow. Andreason can't hit that way; he hits around ninety a minute, but it's just a tick, tick, tick."

"But he must be doing something right," I said. "He's the reigning Nevada state champion."

"I know he drills the year round," said Louis. "Day in and day out. He jogs and does everything, you know. And here I go down to Reno, I spend two or three weeks there horsing around. I'd be out all night, and that's where I got my training. But this year, I've got to be completely different."

"Are you going to take up jogging?"

"Well . . . I just . . . I won't do any jogging or anything like that. I'll just kind of every day hammer and get my arm in shape."

"I saw this black box
with two little funny poles
sticking out of it. I put
a file that I had found
across it, and it hissed and
it sparked and I saw these
beautiful glorious blue
sparks come flying out.
And I said,
'Wow, what a toy!'"

— Robert K. Golka

CHAPTER EIGHT

Sparks of Genius

I found myself spending more and more time at Deputy Dump's shack, which by now had become like a second home. Over the years Floyd had made a number of improvements, adding on a guest room and installing a bathroom complete with a flush toilet— an astonishing feat in view of the fact his house had no plumbing. And now I noticed that he had electric lights and a black-and-white television set.

"For a TV that just come offa a dump, I'm tellin' ya, it's a damn nice little TV," Floyd declared. "All I had to do was put a little tube in it. The guy says, 'It'll talk, but there's no picture.'

"And I says, 'Picture tube?'

"And he says, 'I guess it is, 'cause you cain't get no picture on it. It's black.' He says, 'It's bound to be gone.'

"Well, I didn't say a damn word. I says, 'I'll take it down and play with it. Anyways, I can get a couple of pounds of copper out of it.'

"So I packed it down here, and that evening, why, I set it down. I took the back off'n it, and I turned the TV on. I seen the picture tube light up. *Ah-HAH!* When he said the picture tube was black, I figured what it was right then. So I just looked around for the vertical tube; I pulled it out and looked at the number of it, went

in to my tube box—I got a whole box of tubes back there—and I poked one into it. *Booo*! I had a picture!"

How had he come to know so much about the inner workings of a television set, I wondered? Without missing a beat, Floyd answered that he had studied electronics in Mexico City. It was a required course for all International Rangers.

"We didn't have no TVs, but we had radios. We had a teletype machine. I had a damn teletype machine *and* a telegraph. Took up one whole side of the office."

Eaton hastened to add that he rarely turned his TV set on—no more than ten or fifteen minutes per day.

"I don't mind settin' here in the evenin', havin' a smoke, maybe a cup of coffee, and watchin' the news," he explained. "I like to watch the news, because they show the scenes of what's happening. Or happened. I don't mind watchin' it fer a few minutes—but hell, to just set and glue your eye on that goddamn thang for hours and hours and hours at a time watchin' one thang right after another. Watchin' ball games, soap operas, damn love stories—why, that's just a idiot box."

Eaton had another good reason for not watching too much television: the rising cost of gasoline. The electricity his set ran on was generated by a gas-fueled power plant—what looked to be the front end of a Mazda automobile hooked up to a war surplus AC generator. It was crude but also ingenious, and I couldn't help wondering if the art of transforming old cars into generators was still another of the many skills Floyd had acquired during his tenure as an International Ranger.

"Nope," he answered. The power plant was the work of a friend of his, he said—a scientist named Doctor Golka, who operated a top secret laboratory inside an aircraft hangar on the old air base. There, said Eaton, Dr. Golka had built a device that generated lightning bolts. The biggest lightning bolts ever created by man.

"Uh huh," I nodded. It was exactly the sort of cockamamie tall tale I had come to expect from Floyd—the only difference being that this one was going to be easy to debunk. All I had to do was visit the old air base and see this so-called lightning machine for myself.

To my utter amazement, I soon discovered that everything Floyd had told me was true—except the part about Robert K. Golka holding a Ph.D. In fact, he was a college dropout.

The building he'd taken over—the so-called Enola Gay Hangar—was the largest structure on the base. Parked at the hangar's southeast corner was a tiny house trailer emblazoned on one side with a jagged lightning bolt. There I met up with the thirty-something scientist, who wore a military flight jacket with lightning bolt emblems affixed to the sleeves. I also became acquainted with Bob's two dogs, Doctor Proton and Nitro, and his live-in girlfriend, Agnes Moon. Agnes was a buxom, white-haired matron at least twice as old as her lover—an age difference that never failed to set local tongues wagging. Agnes stood accused of robbing the cradle, Bob of robbing the grave.

The better I got to know Agnes, the more I liked her. She had the sweet disposition of an angel and the maternal instincts of a mother hen. She was constantly after Robert to cut back on his sugar intake, pick up his things, mind his manners, and keep his shirt on in public places.

Not that Robert Golka ever heeded her advice. What others might think of him was of no concern; all that mattered was his quest to tame lightning—what he called "sparks."

Golka told me he'd been obsessed by sparks since the age of five. "I was walking in back of this gas station, pulling a little cart behind me, and I saw this black box with two little funny poles sticking out of it, and three little caps. And I put a file that I had found—there was a bunch of junk in back of the station—I put a file across it, and it hissed and it sparked, and I saw these beautiful, glorious blue sparks come flying out of it. And I said, 'Wow, what a toy!'"

Bob had grown up in Brockton, Massachusetts, and had studied briefly at Northeastern University. He dropped out after becoming obsessed with the life and work of the Croatian-born genius Nikola Tesla, who first conceived the rotating magnetic field upon which virtually all commercial electrical systems in use today are based.

Tesla was a visionary light years ahead of his scientific contemporaries—including Thomas Edison, in whose Menlo Park laboratory he briefly labored. Early in his career, Tesla filed patents for alternating current dynamos, transformers, and motors—patents that would have made him fabulously wealthy had he not foolishly sold them to George Westinghouse for what amounted to peanuts.

In 1899, Nikola Tesla moved west to Colorado Springs, where he built a high frequency resonant transformer, or Tesla coil, with which he reportedly was able to create lightning bolts over a hundred feet in length. He entertained grand plans for his transformer, predicting that one day it might be used to transmit electrical energy through the air without benefit of wires. He also envisioned a handheld oscillator with which one could shake apart a skyscraper, and he sketched a diagram for a death ray capable of zapping incoming intercontinental missiles (yet to be invented) out of the sky. About the same time, he began receiving "signals" from other planets.

As Tesla grew increasingly eccentric, he found it more and more difficult to attract financial backing. In 1943, he died alone in his New York City hotel room, penniless and unheralded except in his native country. Since his death, a cult following has sprung up, a loosely-knit group of free thinkers known as Teslaphiles.

As I read up on the life and times of Nikola Tesla, I was immediately struck by certain parallels. The similarity between the names Golka and Tesla, for instance, and the fact that both men were social misfits whose career paths trended from east to west.

Tesla had moved to the Colorado Rockies because that's where some of the most powerful electrical storms in the country take place. Golka had been drawn to the Bonneville Salt Flats because he was looking for optimum ground conductivity. Another reason for Golka's departure from his hometown: neighbors were threatening to take legal action because his ten-foot Tesla coil was scrambling their television reception.

His first summer in Wendover, Robert Golka had lived and worked alone on the salt flats, with no one for company save his dogs—Doctor Proton, Nitro, and the late Commander Klystron. In the spring of 1974, he finagled a research grant from the U.S. Air Force to study the effects of lightning strikes on aircraft. As a condition of the grant, the Air Force agreed to lease him the Enola Gay hangar for one nominal dollar a year and look the other way should he find any useful war surplus components lying about. The older the components, the better, as far as Bob Golka was concerned. After all, he *was* attempting to replicate a turn-of-the-century science experiment.

In short order, Golka succeeded in filling the entire 60,000-square-foot hangar with *stuff*, including such things as a forklift; a piano; a pinball machine; a jukebox; an oscilloscope; a perambulator-mounted battery charger; and a truck-mounted, 150,000-watt, diesel-fueled generator. Occupying center stage was a 50-foot in diameter corral formed of PVC pipe strung with inch-thick copper cable—what Golka called his "primary" coil. From the primary coil, an overhead wire led to the secondary coil, 30 feet tall and eight feet around. By the time the electrical charge had spiraled to the top of the secondary coil, it would be amplified to a sizzling twenty million volts. No wire can contain such voltage, hence the spectacular electrical discharge we know as lightning.

It was the largest Tesla coil ever built, Golka insisted, and you didn't have to see it in action to sense it was dangerous. The apparatus included a commutator switch in the form of a large metal disk rimmed with teeth like those of a sawmill blade. The disk was attached by a shaft to a motor and spun at such tremendous speed that, were it to break loose from its moorings and sail off in the direction of the StateLine Casino, it would become the roulette wheel from hell. Against such an eventuality, Golka had positioned junk cars on either side of it—including a '49 Chevy coupe I recognized as one half of Two Car Bob's motor pool.

Once, the disk *had* broken loose and disintegrated. Metal fragments had perforated the hangar roof and torn into a heavy-duty transformer, which had leaked several gallons of oil laced with toxic polychlorinated biphenyl onto the concrete floor. For Robert Golka, it was just a typical day in the lab.

Although fascinated by all types of lightning, Golka was intrigued most with a seldom-seen form known as ball lightning. Described as a glowing sphere that infrequently materializes during electrical storms, ball lightning has also been generated accidentally by the diesel-electric power plants of locomotives and submarines. Nikola Tesla claimed to have created ball lightning at will with his Colorado Springs coil. Unfortunately, Tesla's handwritten lab notes are sketchy and all but illegible.

Golka believed ball lightning to be very hot plasma contained within its own magnetic field. That being the case, he postulated that such an energy field might be employed to harness the force of nuclear fusion. The result would be a cheap, safe, and virtually limitless energy source for the future.

Try as I might, I've never been able to gain more than the feeblest understanding of physics and thermodynamics. That portion of my brain which governs scientific thought is evidently stunted—in large part because my high school science teacher was also the varsity football coach. Ever since the fateful day Coach Howard was struck and killed by a lightning bolt while standing on the fifty-yard line, however, I've had a keen interest in high voltage discharges and their practical potential.

Of course, I was also itching to see the fireworks display. For that, Robert Golka explained, I'd have to wait until after dark. In the meantime, he had a pressing matter to attend to. The windshield washer on his 20-year-old Chevy was on the fritz and Bob was determined to bring it back on line—in defiance of a natural law that dictates *no* car's windshield washer ever works after 20 years.

I killed time exploring Golka's sprawling laboratory astride an old bicycle I found. In a far corner of the hangar, I discovered a washroom that, from the looks of it, hadn't been used since V-J Day. It was an eerie feeling to gaze upon the historic ceramic fixtures where once had perched the crew of the Enola Gay. To touch the yellowed, parchment-thin, single-ply, government-issue toilet paper. To flip the same toilet lever bombardier Tom Ferebee had flipped, prior to taking off for Tinian.

Outside, I traced figure eights on the vast tarmac and peddled to the far end of the 9000-foot main runway, passing along the way numerous reinforced-concrete igloos, steel blast doors locked tight, their contents a mystery.

By and by, the sun sank redly behind the Goshute Mountains and Wendover's neon skyline blinked on. The Chevy's windshield washer had miraculously come on line; however, a new crisis had erupted at the nearby Hideaway Club, where the Wurlitzer jukebox had ceased wurlitzing. The entire entourage—Golka, Agnes Moon, Deputy Dump, Deputy Dog, Doctor Proton, Nitro, and myself—set out to have a look.

It took Bob all of thirty seconds to diagnose the problem, another half hour to fix it. Clearly, I thought, here was a man who could earn a good living as a troubleshooter if he chose to. Any type of machine—be it a forklift, arc welder, jukebox, or jack-in-the-box—Bob Golka instinctively knew how it worked. No doubt a lot of folks back in Massachusetts were scratching their heads, wondering why he had walked away from a high-paying job designing computer peripheral systems in order to repair jukeboxes in Nevada.

"I coulda made a lot more money outta that than this," Bob confessed. "I was tying in a computer to monitor a laboratory experiment, building a drinkometer for moneys—tryin' to ingest alcohol into monkeys. See, monkeys are smarter than humans; they won't drink alcohol unless you force-feed 'em."

From the Hideaway Club we migrated to the StateLine Casino, where cocktail waitresses wearing miniskirts and fishnet stockings proceeded to force-feed us alcohol. The drinks were on the house because we were playing the slots. As usual, I wasn't having much luck.

"Let me show you how," said Golka, reaching over and yanking hard on the handle. The reels spun; a plum, an orange, and a bar lined up. The bell clanged, and the machine coughed up twenty nickels.

"Huh? How did you *do* that?" I looked around, but Golka had disappeared. When I caught up with him, he was doing his best to engage an attractive young keno runner in a discussion of particle beam physics.

CHAPTER NINE

One Car Bob

Were space aliens ever to touch down in Nevada, I suspect they'd make their presence known not by tramping out crop circles, but rather by rearranging roadside litter into geometrical patterns such as the one that caught my eye as I sped south on State Route 341 one warm and sunny afternoon in the spring of 1977. I'd spent the morning in crowded Virginia City and was looking forward to escaping into open country. That's when I spotted the supernatural arrangement of beer cans and bottles—and , of course, I had no choice but to stop and investigate.

Not until after I'd climbed out of my van did I realize the entire ravine was under cultivation. "The banana belt of the Comstock" is how resident gardener Bob McKinney described Gold Canyon.

McKinney's was unlike any garden I'd ever seen. Instead of mounds and furrows, it consisted of soft drink bottles, beer cans, Styrofoam cups, wine jugs, milk cartons, sardine tins, and aluminum snack trays. Anything that would hold dirt had been converted into a planter.

I learned that McKinney, age 32, was a native of California and a military veteran. Following his discharge, he'd drifted around the West, touching down briefly in Tucson and Tahoe before settling in Virginia City. There, he'd worked various odd jobs until being "kicked out" of town. He'd rolled downhill, passing through Gold Hill and Silver City before coming to a stop at an abandoned mine just across the road and upslope from his current location.

"That's the best place around," he declared. "See that head frame up there? It's not very far away, but if you're livin' there, it's quiet. You don't hear any traffic, but if you *want* to hear traffic—you know, if you get lonesome—all you have to do is walk over to that hill in front of the head frame. You walk over there and sit down, you look down on the traffic and hear the cars go by, and it's nice."

McKinney had squatted at the mine site for four years, until the owner came along and gave him the boot. Once again at the mercy of gravity, Bob went "straight downhill" to the bottom of Gold Canyon. So now instead of looking down on others, others looked down on him, and there was no escape from the incessant traffic noise.

"You notice how *loud* it is? I get pissed off underneath here, listenin' to 'em. What I do, like for therapy, is walk down the highway awhile, and I walk *beside* the cars. And when I'm standin' up, see, my head's actually higher than people goin' by, and then I make friends again, and I can turn around and come back down here. But pretty soon it starts buildin' up again, and I get pissed off. I like bein' beside 'em or above 'em; I can deal with that. But down here I can't. I'm at their mercy."

Using materials salvaged from the Silver City dump, Bob had built himself a one-room shack, but then one day he wandered off and forgot to douse the fire in his fireplace. When he returned, the fire department was parked where his house used to be.

McKinney moved into his car, a 1961 Ford Galaxie. He slept in the back seat, which was uncomfortable because he had no room to stretch out his long legs. Often at night, he'd feel a charley horse coming on. "And if it starts up, I gotta open the door quickly and straighten my leg before it really gets goin', or I'll be in agony."

The Galaxie's trunk was crammed full of science fiction paperbacks, Bob's favorite authors being Isaac Asimov, Arthur C. Clarke, and J.R.R. Tolkien. He also enjoyed Beverly Cleary's *The Mouse and the Motorcycle*. Pornography did nothing for him, he said, nor had he been able to finish *Helter Skelter*.

Bob McKinney's humble home furnishings radiated outward from the Galaxie in concentric circles like the June Taylor Dancers. His pantry was a cardboard box; the trunks of nearby cottonwoods served as conceptual walls upon which hung his overcoat, umbrella, and a dartboard.

"If I had the car goin' and licensed—and myself—and had gas in the tank, I'd probably go to Tahoe," he told me. "Over in those mountains it's a different deal. It's the next step up."

To occupy his empty hours, McKinney had taken up gardening, using containers he found along the road for planters and seeds salvaged from the Silver City dump. Dirt was easy to come by. Water, however, entailed a mile-long hike to the nearest spring.

"I haul it up, two or three gallons at a time—mainly for me, but then I share it with them."

He'd tried growing a variety of crops: grapes, potatoes, onions, lettuce, peas, and beans. However, only a handful of seeds had sprouted, and nothing yet had blossomed.

"There's no tellin' which ones go and which ones don't," he said. "It's just one big chance."

The previous spring, the potatoes had started off well, growing to a height of three inches. This year's potato crop had fared even better, growing a full ten inches before falling over dead.

Bob couldn't quite put his finger on the problem—or problems. Seeds sowed in tin cans appeared to do better than those planted in bottles—especially if he remembered to punch holes in the bottoms of the cans. Unfortunately, he seldom remembered to punch those holes. Moreover, it was a challenge keeping track of which plants had been watered and which plants hadn't. Which ones had been fertilized? Most of the time, he couldn't even remember which seeds he'd planted where. On top of everything else, there was the ongoing challenge of putting food and drink on his own makeshift table. And with no income, how was he ever going to get his car up and running and himself back into the high country?

"I'm tryin' to get it outta here," he insisted. "But the goddamn jack won't pick it up. I gotta borrow a big jack and get it up, and then it'll move around."

As he spoke, Bob shuffled from planter to planter, dribbling water into some containers and skipping others altogether. It was hard to know which plants to attend to first, they all looked so desperate.

Bob picked up a gallon jug and poured a pint of muddy water onto the ground. "That's the thing with these bottles," he sighed. "Some of these damn things will have a cuppa water in 'em. I don't know how the rain gets in there—it must aim for it."

Bob held the opaque green glass jug up the sunlight and examined its soupy contents. "I like these bottles," he declared. "If something ever got started in there, I think it'd have a good little time if I didn't add too much water.

"I like the cans because I don't drown 'em, but they go dry. You have to water 'em consistently. Every day you have to . . . "

Something had caught McKinney's eye—a pale greenish-yellow stalk peeping above the rim of a Pringle's potato chip canister.

"There's a little onion," he chirped. "It started out, you know, a regular onion. A little green on it—a good healthy green on it—and then it started to shrink up. I'm tryin' to make it well. I'm hoping I can bring it around.

"Last year I had grapes goin.' They got about an inch high, and that's as far as they went. In that wine bottle, with the sun hittin' it, I guess it was like a magnifyin' glass on 'em. Just absolutely fried 'em out, is what happened."

Bending low to the ground, Bob peered into the mouth of one bottle after another. He shook his head. "Really, I can just imagine what they're goin' through in there. They're being *suffocated!*"

I was beginning to feel a touch of the greenhouse effect myself, and I'd only been parked in Gold Canyon for half an hour. How shall I phrase it? I was beginning to feel all *bottled up* inside.

"Hey!" Bob suddenly exclaimed. "This little guy was hidin' back here behind the label. Yeah, it's probably too hot, so he's growing in the shade down there. That's what he's doin'; he's hidin' from the sun."

Bob was on his hands and knees now, one eye pressed against the mouth of a Vino Fino jug.

"*Goddamn!* I don't know what this one is. Could be a little *flower!*"

"Up until then I thought he was just a wino. When he told me he was Howard Hughes, I thought, "Wow, this guy's really squirrelly. He's been out here a little too long.""

— Melvin Dummar

CHAPTER TEN

Pennies from Heaven

I picked up a couple of girls one time, they wanted me to take 'em to San Francisco. They wanted to join that flower movement or whatever it was there in San Francisco. And if I'd ahad a little more money, I'd probably have taken 'em with me.

I picked up another girl one time—I always used to look for them good-lookin' girls hitchhikin'—and I picked up one girl, she had a big sack, and she started pullin' things outta the sack and tellin' me about where she got 'em. Where she'd stole this and where she'd stole that. She was like a kleptomaniac, I guess. She was tellin' me she'd stole this blouse at such and such a store, and stole somethin' else here, and I just looked at her, and I says, "Young lady, how do you know that I'm not a police officer? You just get in the car, you don't know who I am at all, and you're tellin' me about all this stuff you've been stealing." I got rid of her pretty fast. She was a little weird, that girl was.

—Melvin Dummar

By now, I'd spent so much time roaming the parallel universe of Nevada that when I heard the Silver State's richest resident had died and left millions of dollars to a stranger whose name he couldn't even spell, I actually *believed* it. I mean, how was it any different from the multitude of get-rich-quick fantasies I'd seen depicted on billboards promoting legalized gambling?

Melvin Dummar had grown up in the shadow of those same billboards, and, as a boy, had watched in wide-eyed wonder as the stretch limos roared past his father's humble mining claim in Fairfield. Land yachts they were, with tinted windows and air-conditioned interiors upholstered in fine leather and furnished with silicone-implanted showgirls. A suitcase stuffed with non-sequential, high-denomination bills in the trunk. Elvis on the radio!

It was a way of life young Melvin could only dream about. But now things were about to change. Eccentric billionaire Howard

Robard Hughes had expired aboard his private jet in the sky above Mexico, and Melvin's life would never be the same.

On the day Howard Hughes died, Melvin, his second wife Bonnie, and four of their children were living in a cramped apartment above a gas station they leased in Willard—a sleepy northern Utah settlement named after Willard Richards, an early day Mormon pioneer and counselor to Brigham Young. Recently bypassed by Interstate 15, Willard had experienced a sharp decline in traffic and a commensurate decline in commerce. The struggling business district consisted mostly of seasonal farm produce stands, a restaurant, Mel's gas station, and Utah's largest war surplus emporium. News of Hughes' death caused nary an uptick on the local business barometer.

Three uneventful weeks passed after Howard Hughes' death. Then, a mysterious, blue Mercedes sedan pulled into the station. Shortly afterward, Melvin discovered a brown manila envelope lying on his desk. The envelope wasn't addressed to him, but no matter—Melvin opened it anyway. Inside, he found a three-page, 261-word, hand-written document: The Last Will and Testament of Howard Robard Hughes.

To Melvin's astonishment, he saw that among the twelve beneficiaries was a "Melvin DuMar of Gabbs, Nevada."

Melvin wasn't sure what to do next. He'd never been named in a will before, and his knowledge of how the legal system worked was limited. Perhaps he shouldn't have opened the envelope in the first place. After all, it *had* been addressed to David O. McKay, late president of the Mormon Church.

Melvin slipped the will back into the envelope and carefully resealed it. He tried to think: Who is the *current* president of the Mormon Church?

I picked up one guy; he actually wasn't hitchhiking. He was lost; in fact, he was in hysterics. It was up near Ione, here in Nevada. I guess

he'd been out there for a couple of days. It was raining and I was just drivin'—I had a dune buggy, or a car that I'd cut down—and I was drivin' up this dirt road near Ione, and I seen this guy runnin' down the side of the hill through the sagebrush, screamin' and hollerin,' so I stopped to see what his problem was.

And he just said, "Oh my God, please take me to civilization!"

He was all cut up and bleeding. His shirt, coat, and everything was all ripped up. I guess he'd been out there for a couple of days lost, deer hunting. He was from Southern California. I put him in my dune buggy and took him back to Ione. They had a search party there, but they were all settin' around the bar drinking. I pulled up and the guy got out and—I can't remember what his name was, but somebody said, "Well, here's Joe now! Hey, we found him!" And those guys were settin' around drinkin', havin' a party. Nobody was even out lookin' for him.

Soon as Bonnie returned to the gas station that afternoon, Melvin jumped into the family car and drove straight to Temple Square in Salt Lake City. There he was informed that the current leader of the Church of Jesus Christ of Latter-day Saints was Spencer W. Kimball, and that Kimball's office was on the 25th floor of the church office building. When Melvin stepped off the elevator, however, the receptionist informed him that President Kimball was in a meeting. Melvin made his way down a hallway to a restroom, where he stuffed the will inside a second envelope, along with a note that read: "This was found by Joseph Smith's house in 1972—thought you might be interested." He addressed the outer envelope to President Kimball, tossed it onto a nearby desk, and dashed out the door.

In the movie they have me drivin' a pickup, but when I picked him up, I was actually driving a '66 Chevrolet Caprice. I think it was either on the 29th or the 30th of December 1967. He was lying about a hundred yards off the main highway on sort of a dirt road. Looked like, appeared to me like somebody'd dumped him out there, 'cause he was lying on the ground. When I first seen him with my headlights I thought he was dead. But then I seen him moving and trying to get up, so that's when I went over and helped him get up. Took him back over to the car and put him in the car. He was just trembling all over—shaking. He was trembling like he was either cold or he was afraid of me. Or something.

When Spencer Kimball opened the envelope, he was indeed interested, because, according to the enclosed will, Howard Hughes had bequeathed one-sixteenth of his immense fortune to the Mormon Church. Two days later, a delegation of Latter-day Saint lawyers boarded a plane for Las Vegas, where they presented the curious document to a Clark County district judge. The following morning, Bonnie Dummar looked out her front window and saw an advancing army of cameramen and reporters.

I was with him maybe two hours, give or take a few minutes. And after he was with me for awhile, we were talkin' about different things I was doin'. Where I was workin'. And I think we were talking about the aircraft industry, because I'd been in the Air Force. And after I got out of the Air Force, just before I got married, I was trying to get a job in some of the aircraft plants. He said he was familiar with Hughes Aircraft because he owned it. And that's when he told me he was Howard Hughes. Up until then I thought he was just a wino. In fact, I still thought he was a wino after that. When he told me he was Howard Hughes. I thought, "Wow, this guy's really squirrelly. He's been out here a little too long."

The squirrelly stranger asked to be dropped off behind the Sands Hotel in Las Vegas, Melvin would later tell the court. In parting, Hughes had asked Melvin if he had any spare change, and Melvin had tossed him a quarter—never dreaming that in only nine short years his two-bit investment would appreciate to over 156 million dollars!

The media swallowed the story hook, line, and sinker—and so did the reading public. For it was more than just news; it was the stuff of parable. Overnight, Melvin Dummar became America's blue-collar folk hero, the only working stiff in history ever to benefit from trickle-down economics.

But as the Dummars soon found out, even the demise of a billionaire benefactor has a downside. As news of Melvin's windfall spread, distant relatives and newfound friends began to surface. Well-wishers from around the globe telephoned to offer congratulations and investment advice. Wackos applied for loans in order to finance wacky schemes. Reporters and photographers of every stripe beat a path to their door; TV vans lined the highway and blocked the entrance to the station. Instead of pumping gas, Bonnie and Melvin found themselves being continually pumped for information. In coffee shops all up and down U.S. 89, the overworked and underpaid were raising toasts to their heretofore obscure blue collar hero.

Meantime, back in Las Vegas, the so-called "Mormon Will" had been undergoing intense forensic scrutiny, and already a number of irregularities had surfaced. Why, the investigators wondered, had Hughes bequeathed his Hercules flying boat to the city of Long Beach when, at the time the will was allegedly written, he no longer owned it? And why had he referred to the HK-1 as the Spruce Goose—a derogatory nickname he hated? How was it that the heretofore meticulous Hughes had managed to misspell better than one in every twenty words—including "Las Vagas," the city that had been his legal residence since 1966?

In terms of comparative literary merit, the fictitious Hughes autobiography penned a few years earlier by Clifford Irving was a masterpiece. Still, seven months would pass and millions of dollars in court costs be consumed before finally the will was pronounced a fake. Yet unlike Irving, who went to jail, Melvin Dummar was never convicted of fraud. Moreover, if a valid Howard Hughes will does exist, it has never been found.

Three years later, the "love story" of Melvin and Howard was turned into a Hollywood movie, for which screenwriter Bo Goldman and supporting actress Mary Steenburgen would each win Academy Awards. Directed by Jonathan Demme, *Melvin and Howard* features the real Melvin Dummar in his first ever dramatic role—a bit part as a soda jerk for which he receives a seven-dollar royalty whenever the film is shown on television.

Six months after the film's premier at Sundance and four years after Howard Hughes stopped breathing, Melvin had given up both acting and pumping gas and was eking out a living as a frozen fish salesman in Utah and Nevada. He was also involved in the "multilevel marketing" of a powdered milk substitute—not to be confused, he hastened to add, with a pyramid scheme.

His overriding ambition, however, was to make it big as a lounge singer. To that end he had retained a manager and assembled a band, "Melvin and Revival," and was looking forward to the release of his first album. Among the cuts would be several of his own compositions—topical ballads such as "American Dreamer" and "Thank You, Howard." And, of course, the Christmas carol featured in Demme's movie: "Santa's Souped-Up Sleigh."

I had met Melvin briefly at a party and was hoping to get to know him better. Happily, one day Bonnie called to announce she was driving out to Gabbs, Nevada, to join Melvin for the weekend. Would I care to tag along?

The two of us left Salt Lake City on a Friday at about four in the afternoon. Traveling as I normally do, by Volkswagen bus, I'd have expected to reach Gabbs by Monday afternoon. Bonnie was thinking we might get there before dark.

By the time we blew into Elko, night had long since fallen. Seventy-two miles farther down the road in Battle Mountain, we made a ninety-degree turn. This put us on State Route 305, which runs south toward Austin, roughly parallel to the imaginary Reese River. I was behind the wheel now, and for the next 80 miles, I didn't see a single headlight. We did, however, have close encounters with three range cows, two coyotes, a small herd of pronghorns, two dozen jackrabbits, a bobcat, and an owl.

I don't recall pulling into Gabbs; I only remember waking up the following morning. I was tucked inside my sleeping bag, naked except for my undershorts, stretched out upon a Mediterranean-style, crushed velvet sofa. Saturday morning cartoons played on a nearby television set; a young girl sat cross-legged on the lime-green shag carpeting, oblivious to the stranger encamped on her sofa.

I learned later I was in the home of Melvin's brother Ray, who at the time was police chief of Gabbs. Parked in the yard behind Ray's house was an authentic historical artifact: the rusting chassis of the milk truck in which newlyweds Melvin and Bonnie had fled the "weirdness" of Southern California.

Following breakfast, Melvin, Bonnie, and I set out in Mel's company car, a compact Mercury Bobcat. Ostensibly, we were out to enlist new distributors for the artificial powdered milk product that was poised to revolutionize the nondairy industry. After just one unsuccessful sales call, however, Mel lost interest. We decided we'd pay a visit to the nearby Berlin-Ichthyosaur State Park.

Berlin is a silver boomtown that flourished briefly around the turn of the century; the ichthyosaur was a prehistoric aquatic creature that lived 180 million years ago, at a time when most of Nevada lay at the bottom of a vast inland sea. Over 30 fossilized skeletons of the giant "fish lizards" have been quarried from the area, three of which are on public display.

"*Help! Help!*" cried Bonnie, who had jammed her hand inside the maw of a fossilized fish lizard and was pretending to be trapped. Ignoring her cries, Melvin and I went over the fine points of his disputed relationship to the deceased Howard Hughes.

"Did anyone ever give you a lie detector test?" I asked.

"It got so bad there for awhile," Melvin replied, "that everything I'd say, it'd seem like they'd wanna give me another polyagraph test. I got so sick of it that I hated to talk to anybody. I didn't want to say nothin' to nobody, because everything I'd say, I was being misquoted and misinterpreted. Finally one time I was in there at the University of Utah with Dr. David Raskin. He asked me two or three different questions, and then he turned the machine off and come runnin' in and said he thought I'd died, because he couldn't get a reaction of any kind. Because I was just completely wore out. It was like I almost lost my will to live, because of so many people badgering me and harassing me and askin' me and everything."

Presently we were westbound on State Route 844. Bonnie had freed herself from the jaws of the prehistoric ichthyosaur and Melvin was behind the Bobcat's wheel. I noticed that he kept one eye trained on the shoulder at all times—a lifelong habit, he explained. A lot of useful stuff falls off trucks—such things as wrenches and screwdrivers, bungee cords and folding aluminum law chairs. Once he'd even come upon a cardboard box filled with brand-new, stuffed teddy bears.

If Melvin Dummar is good at finding stuff, he's also good at winning stuff. Back when he lived in Southern California, he'd demonstrated a knack for getting himself onto television game shows. He has appeared on both *The New Price Is Right* and *Hollywood Squares*, and, on three separate occasions, was a contestant on *Let's Make a Deal*. Host Monte Hall hadn't recognized him because the first time around Mel had been disguised as a hobo; the second time, a bunch of oranges. The *third* time, not only had Melvin changed his costume, but his name as well.

"I won on *Let's Make a Deal* twice as Melvin Dummar," he explained, "and then there was other people wanted me to go on and win prizes for them. And so I went on *Let's Make a Deal* several times using other people's names and won prizes."

"But didn't you sign an agreement to the effect that you hadn't appeared on the program before?" I asked.

"Uh huh."

"So wasn't what you did against the rules?"

"Yes, it was. In fact, I kinda feel sorry, you know, for doing it. Because they used that in court against me—saying I was a con man and everything, which I really wasn't. I was just doing it for fun. And because some of these other people, such as my ex-father-in-law, he wanted to win a prize and all that. But he was just too embarrassed. He said he didn't want to go down there and make a fool of himself. Said he wanted me to go down and do it for him.

"So I said, 'Well, I'll go down there and win you something. But I'll use your name, your social security card, your address, and whatever I win goes to you.'

"You know, I just did it for the heck of it, and I didn't tell him he had to give me anything at all. But when he won the new car, he gave me his old one. He had a '68 Ford LTD, and I took the LTD down and traded it in as the down payment on the El Dorado Convertible."

"Which in the movie was repossessed after you fell behind in the payments."

"Yeah. Well, they make it appear in the movie that I don't ever pay my bills and stuff. That I've had one car repossessed right after another and everything else. I've had (laughs) quite a few cars repossessed, but under different circumstances than what the movie depicts.

"I had one car repossessed because I got so stupid I just gave it to a guy to take over the payments, and I didn't have it changed into his name. And actually, I've done that with two different cars, just turned it over to somebody and never seen to it that it was changed into their name. One guy, after I let him have it—a 1965 Pontiac—he paid on it for two or three months, and then he just stopped paying on it, and the bank repossessed it.

"And then the '71 El Dorado convertible, I let a guy just take over the payments, but he never made a single payment. I'd talk to him, I phoned, but I never could run him down, and finally the bank caught up with him and repossessed it. Of course, it was in my name, so it kinda ruined my credit."

That was how things usually went. Melvin would start out with the purest of intentions only to wind up in trouble—all because of other irresponsible people.

We were now on U.S. 50, speeding toward Fallon, where Melvin had attended high school and where the story of his life was currently playing at the local movie house. Given that Melvin Dummar was Fallon's most famous native son, it occurred to me he should be arriving by chauffeured limousine—not in a Mercury Bobcat.

Had it been a Greek play instead of a Hollywood production, surely the story of Melvin Dummar would have played out differently. In the Greek version, just when Melvin's situation appeared utterly hopeless, Howard Hughes would be lowered to the stage on a rope. Melvin would be snatched from the clutches of his creditors and carried off to a penthouse suite high atop the Desert Inn—far, far removed from the harsh realities of the workaday world.

"I never *really* thought I'd ever get it," sighed Melvin. "Oh, a few times, I *did* think about it. If by some miracle we ever did see any of the money, I'd probably invest most of it in real estate. And I also like to travel. I really love to travel and go around. Of course, I like to hunt and fish an awful lot, too. If I had the money, I would undoubtedly do a lot of hunting and fishing. I would love to entertain. I'd love to be a singer and just entertain people. And sports, too; I really like sports. I think if I had the money, I would probably get involved in some of the things that I've always wanted to do, like skydiving and hang gliding. And maybe auto racing . . . "

"And *suicide*," chirped Bonnie from the back seat.

Did he ever wish, I wondered, that he had handled things differently?

"Well, if I had it to do all over again, I'd probably do the same thing. You know, as far as helping him—if I found somebody that was in trouble, like Hughes was, I'd still help him.

"I think it was kinda neat that he left me in his will and everything and remembered me. But I only wish that he'd have handled it different and had filed in court himself, or had his attorneys do it, or had it notarized, or whatever it is they do to 'em, instead of dropping it off like he did, so everything wouldn't be fallin' on me. And accusing me and my whole family, friends, neighbors, and everybody else of having a big plot or scheme going—that's what *really* hurt."

"If you just put your
mind to it, you kin visit
anywheres in the world
you want to at night.
All you gotta do
is let your mind wander."

— Floyd Eaton

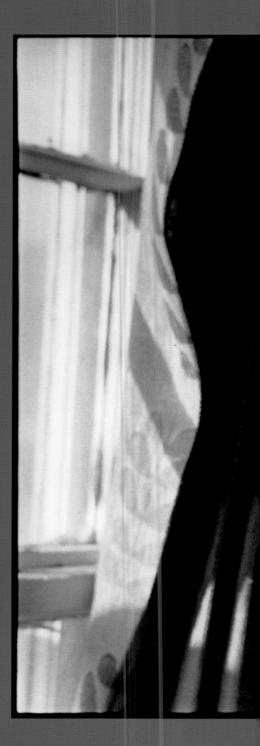

CHAPTER ELEVEN

Going South

The 1980s were upon us. Times were changing, and it was fast becoming clear that the existential wonderland of a rabbit hole I'd fallen into ten years earlier was about to change as well. Nevada was entering upon yet another new boom phase; in fact, it would soon become the fastest-growing state in the nation. This was good news for some, but not for everyone.

Thanks to soaring gold prices and new recovery technologies, mining claims throughout the mineral belt were being reactivated. Ghost towns were stirring back to life and long-dormant dogs being evicted from previously vacant storefronts. Low-margin shopkeepers like Mom Pavlakis and Jack Killinger were being squeezed out of business; cantankerous caretakers like Ray Walker were no longer in demand. Ely got a Motel 6 and then a McDonald's.

In West Wendover, new casinos, housing developments and a golf course were springing up on land that had previously been the exclusive domain of jackrabbits and scorpions. A brand new sewage treatment plant was under construction, and bulldozers were clearing brush for what would soon become the town's first sanitary landfill.

Floyd Eaton didn't care for that word—sanitary. Even more distressing, the new landfill would be situated on the Utah side of town. No way Floyd could ever adjust to living in Utah. "Too many rules and regulations to suit me," he groused.

As his trash flow began to dry up, Floyd's thoughts increasingly turned homeward, to that storied land below the Mason-Dixon Line where rattlesnake melons grow wild and every other tree shelters a tasty raccoon. In Dixie he wouldn't need money; he could fish and hunt and live off the bounty of the land—same as when he was a young boy growing up along the banks of the Mississippi River. Then October arrived; lenticular clouds hovered low over the Goshute Mountains and a chilly wind blew in from the northwest. As he had so many times before, Eaton set about packing his bindle bag. He pulled on his pointy-toed Justin boots, grabbed his hat, and whistled for Tina. Together, the pair strode through the sagebrush to Highway 93. Floyd stuck out his thumb.

Days later, I received a letter postmarked Baker, Nevada. Some miles outside of Ely, Floyd had hitched a ride with a brand inspector by the name of Robison. It happened that Mr. Robison was in need of a caretaker to look after a property he owned at the foot of Wheeler Peak. Did Eaton want a job?

"It's doubtful that I shall remain here longer than a couple more months," Eaton's letter continued. "It snows too much this high to suit my fancy. If it's possible and the Lord's willing, I'm going to relocate somewhere down in the southern country where I shall be able to do a little fishing and hunting to have those things to eat you've heard me speak of so often."

The letter included directions to the Robison Ranch, and soon I found myself heading west on Highway 50, holding the steering wheel in one hand and Floyd's crudely drawn map in the other. I was looking forward to seeing my old friend Floyd again—no longer a desert rat but now a mountain man.

Rising more than thirteen thousand feet above sea level, Wheeler Peak is the tallest mountain in the Snake Range and the second highest elevation in Nevada. In a sheltered cirque below its windswept summit can be found the Great Basin's only active glacier. At timberline grow ancient bristlecone pines, some of which were seedlings in the time of the pharaohs. In 1986, Wheeler Peak would become the centerpiece of the nation's 49th national park; however, on this fine fall day Floyd Eaton pretty much had it all to himself.

The Robison "Ranch" was tiny, with only one small, irrigated pasture and an orchard consisting of mostly dead fruit trees. The foursquare-style main house included two bedrooms, one of which was piled from floor to ceiling with back issues of *National Geographic* magazine. The other was furnished with two single beds and dominated by the mounted head of an enormous bull moose.

Eaton's "foreman" job entailed some light maintenance, but for the most part all he had to do was keep an eye on things. The position paid little, and offered nothing in the way of retirement or medical benefits. However, Floyd's employer was a compassionate man, and I soon learned that he had been working quietly behind the scenes to secure a pension for Floyd from the Social Security Administration. Problem was, the federal government had no record of Eaton's *existence*, let alone his employment history.

What did *I* know, Robison asked, about this mysterious hitchhiker he'd picked up in the middle of nowhere?

"Well, he's *not* Howard Hughes," I answered. "And I'm confident he's not running from an ex-wife or the law. If you're asking me if he can be trusted, I can assure you Floyd Eaton is the most honest person I've ever met. That is to say . . . "

"Yeah, I think I know what you're getting at," Robison interrupted. The two of us were standing at the far end of the pasture where Floyd's boss had asked me to accompany him, ostensibly to help move an irrigation pipe.

"I take it then," I said, "he's told you about his career as an International Ranger?"

"Yep."

"And his war record? Did he tell you he once commanded a tank company in North Africa?"

"I thought he had served in the Army Air Corps."

"Oh, he did. But only until his B-17 was shot down over Germany, where he was taken prisoner but managed to escape by impersonating a Nazi officer. He speaks perfect German, you know, with just a slight Cajun accent. And, by the way, are you aware that Elizabeth Taylor's real name is Delores Valdez?"

Robison motioned for me to stop. "Well, I'll tell you what he *has* done," he declared. "He's bullshitted his life away, is what. He's *completely bullshitted his entire life away.*"

I promised Mr. Robison I'd do my best to squeeze some bona fide biographical information out of Floyd. During the days that followed, as my interrogation wore on, a somewhat more plausible biography began to take shape.

I learned that Floyd had been born in 1904 in Point Pleasant, Missouri, in a tent on the banks of the Mississippi River. His mother had given birth to eight children, only two of whom had survived—Floyd and a sister who was married and leading a conventional life in Louisiana.

His father had worked as a commercial fisherman and trapper by day and as a moonshiner by night. The business kept the family on the move, and as a result, Floyd had attended public schools in both Vicksburg and Memphis, advancing only as far as the sixth grade before he was expelled—for smoking a pipe in the classroom, he said. After his folks passed away and during the dust bowl years, Eaton had traveled widely as a hobo, touching down for a time in Texas, where he found work with a traveling carnival.

One evening as we were undressing for bed, I noticed that Floyd wore a corset. It was, he explained, a memento from his carnival days.

"Damn piece of steel rolled off'n a truck on me," he explained. "I was puttin' up one of these mechanical swings—we call 'em mix-ups—and I put the bar, the leg onto it. And another'n on. And then I turned around to do something, and stooped over, and that goddamn thang slipped off the truck and fell over on me. I was stooped over, and it come right down acrost my back."

To the astonishment of everyone watching, Floyd struggled to his feet and resumed putting the ride together. Meantime, witnesses to the accident ran to fetch the boss man, the boss man's wife, and the boss man's brother. Together they hustled Floyd into a car and drove him straight to the nearest hospital.

"I had a little trouble gettin' out of the car when we got there," Floyd recalled, "but I got out, and I walked inta the hospital. And they put me on the extra ray table, took a extra ray."

Eaton paused momentarily to rekindle his Kaywoodie, an action I'd come to recognize as a surefire sign that we were about to veer off into the fiction department.

"The doc, he come in, he says, 'Kin you read a extra ray?'

"I said, 'Yeah, I kin read 'em.'

"The doc, he held one of 'em up. Says, 'Take a look't that one. Tell me what it is.'

"And I looked. I says, 'It's just a clear-cut break, that's all.'

"And he says, 'You're *right*!'

"Wait a minute, Floyd," I interrupted. "If your spinal cord had been severed, you wouldn't be able to walk. You'd have no feeling in your legs, and most likely you'd be sitting in a wheelchair right now."

"Uh huh," Floyd nodded. That's just what the doctor had said—that Floyd's carney career was over, that this time the show would just have to go on without him. However, Floyd would hear none of it.

"'Like *hell*,' I says. 'I gotta goddamn ride down here I gotta operate. I cain't be in no goddamn hospital!'

"And directly a specialist happened to come up. And the specialist says, 'Shit, let me talk t' that guy!'

"And he come in, he looked at that extra ray. He looked at me, and he says, 'They tell me you *walked* in here!'

"And I says, 'Yeah.'

"And he says, 'Kin you git up?'

"I says, 'Yeah. I kin git up.'

"He says, 'Let's *see* you git up.' Says, 'I don't believe, by god, that you kin walk a'tall.' Says, 'By the look of this goddamn thang, you *cain't* walk!'

"So I just eased up and got my feet over on the floor, and put my hand down this way. I put my hands down this way, and by god, I raised myself up off'n that cot. I got straightened up, I walked around the room fer him.

"That doctor looked at the nurse; he says, 'Git him in that bed over yonder.' Says, 'Git him in a bed right quick! I'll be back in just a minute or two.' Says, 'I'm goin' up town.' Directly he come back with one of them thangs right there."

"The doctor went into town and bought you a corset?"

"Yep."

Eaton tossed the girdle aside, switched off the light, and eased himself into the bed next to mine. As my eyes grew accustomed to the dark, I could make out the shaggy outline of the bull moose looming overhead. In the moonlight it was scary—like those mysterious nighttime apparitions that had spooked off all of the ranch's previous caretakers.

"Are *you* afraid of ghosts, Floyd?" I asked.

"Nawww. There's no use t' be scared of a ghost, because a ghost is just the inner soul of somebody that's been dreamin'."

"What are you telling me, Floyd? You mean a ghost isn't the unquiet spirit of a dead person?"

"Nooo. It's just somebody's inner soul, wanderin' around, is all."

"Have you ever seen a ghost, Floyd?"

"I've seen some thangs that was supposed t' been ghosts. I seen my father one time when I was little. Me and my cousin was about three miles from home, walkin' through a field, and there was an old house out there. And my cousin was the first to see it. He just happened t' look up and he seen somebody walkin' behind some bushes. He says, 'Who's that walkin' over yonder?'

"I looked up. I says, 'That's *Dad*!'

"Well, we walked over there. Directly Dad walked inta the old house and we hollered for him t' come out. But he never did answer or nothin'. And when we got back home, there was Dad layin' in the bed, by god, *asleep*. And when he woke up, he says, 'You know, I had a helluva dream awhile ago. By god, I was dreamin' about goin' to an old house, and goin' in it and lookin' around. And,' he says, 'it was a house that was almost fell down, but there was stuff still *in* the old house.'

"I says, '*Describe* that old house.'

"Dad, he described it.

"I says, 'That old house is right down in the field here.'

"Dad, he says, 'Yeah, I know where that old house is.'

"I started laughin'. I says, 'You were *there*, at that old house. Me 'n' Bill saw ya. You was walkin' to the house, and you was dressed, had on the same clothes just like you do right now. Only difference was, you had on that brown and white cap.'

"Dad, he says, 'In my dream, I had on that cap.'"

"So it was your father's spirit that you saw walking in the field?" I asked.

"It was his inner self, just wanderin' around. You know one thang? If you just put yer mind to it, you kin visit anywheres in the world you want to at night. You kin go anywheres you want in the world; all you gotta do is just think about where in the hell you'd like to be, and directly go to bed and let yer mind wander—and by god, it'll *go* there!"

I passed my last wakeful moments thinking of all the places in the world I'd like to visit, all the wonderful things I'd like to see. How I'd love to see the pyramids along the Nile, fly the ocean in a silver plane, smell the marketplace in old Algiers when it's wet with rain . . .

Beside me now I could hear deep breathing, which I took as a sign that Floyd Eaton's inner self had up and wandered off. Tina was snoring as well, and if dogs have inner selves, I'm confident she was at her beloved master's side.

Then gradually I, too, drifted off to dreamland. Next thing I knew I was making my way across a weedy field toward an abandoned farmhouse. On my head was an unfamiliar brown and white cap. I heard a noise behind me. Ever so slowly I turned around—and came face to face with an enormous bull moose!

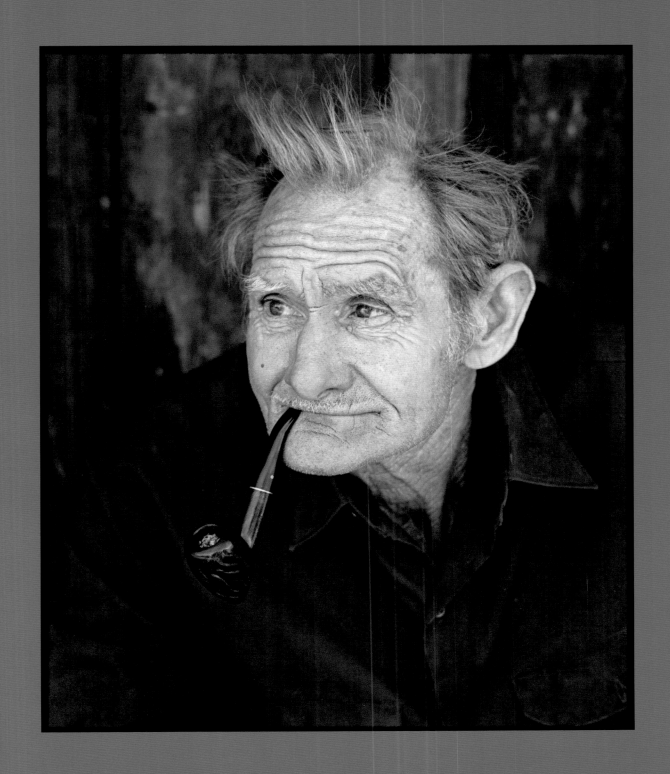